Acknowledgments

I believe that learning to get along and working collectively is a solution to many of our problems, both minor and major, daily and long-term. It is interesting to observe that often, when a problem or catastrophe occurs, the word that is said—and many times shouted—by those involved is "cooperation," not competition or individualization. Whether it be a local food drive for the hungry; a state-wide police search for a missing child; national disasters like the Midwest summer floods, Los Angeles riots, or Florida hurricanes; or the international plea that is regularly made for peace, cooperation is seen as the solution.

The irony is that while we believe that individualization and competition make us strong, they may be the problems. They are certainly not solutions. I hope that by starting with children as the best resource we have, the world can become a place where people work together and bring out the best in each other, thereby resolving differences that currently keep people apart and minimize the collective good.

When I think of who and what influenced my thinking about cooperation, there is a need for acknowledgment. With acknowledgment defined as "expressing appreciation and gratitude," I thank the following individuals for their friendship, professional relationships, and/or writings:

Cooper Wiggen, George Spencer, Harold Mushel, Willy Stitsworth, Joe Walsh, Phyllis Deer, Cal Zweifel, Stan Bezanson, John Mallander, Larry Reed, Dick Bynum, Lyndon Brown, Mara Sapon-Shevin, Ivan Dahl, Marianne Torbert, Terry Orlick, Roger and David Johnson, David Elkind, Spencer Kagan, Alfie Kohn, Jonathan Kozol, Lisbeth Schorr, John Goodlad, Sara Ashworth, and the late Muska Mosston.

I am particularly grateful to the children from Cowern Elementary School, Greenleaf Elementary School, Elm Creek Elementary School, St. Joseph's School, and physical education teacher Joel Saavre and Elementary Avenue Day Care. From these children, I learned about teaching, learning, caring, and laughing. In addition, during my first year of teaching, there was a first grade student named Jenny, to whom I am ever grateful; she taught me the joy of movement, with no strings attached.

I'd also like to extend my thanks to Darel Paulson of Moorhead State University A-V Graphics Department who did the photographic work for this book.

And to Lee, Sara, and Abby—thanks.

This book is dedicated to the task set before us by Sitting Bull, a Lakota Sioux, in 1877. Not only are these words important and challenging, but they remind us that solutions to problems have been around for a long time.

"Let us put our minds together and see what life we can make for our children."

COOPERATIVE
LEARNING
in Physical Education

Steve Grineski, EdD
Moorhead State University

Human Kinetics

Library of Congress Cataloging-in-Publication Data

Grineski, Steve, 1952-
  Cooperative learning in physical education / Steve Grineski.
    p. cm.
  Includes bibliographical references (p.   ) and index.
  ISBN 0-87322-879-0
  1. Physical education and training--United States.   2. Group work
in education--United States.   I. Title.
  GV223.G75   1996
  796'.07'0973--dc20   96-15782
                                                                   CIP

ISBN: 0-87322-879-0

Acquisitions Editor: Rick Frey, PhD; **Developmental Editor:** Elaine Mustain; **Assistant Editors:** Susan Moore-Kruse, Jacqueline Eaton Blakley, and John Wentworth; **Editorial Assistant:** Amy Carnes; **Copyeditor:** Bonnie Pettifor; **Proofreader:** Anne Meyer Byler; **Indexer:** Craig Brown; **Typesetter and Layout Artist:** Francine Hamerski; **Text Designer:** Judy Henderson; **Photo Editor:** Boyd LaFoon; **Cover Designer:** Keith Blomberg; **Photographer (cover and interior):** Darel Paulson; **Illustrator:** Studio 2-D; **Printer:** United Graphics

Printed in the United States of America   10   9   8   7   6   5   4

Human Kinetics
Web site: www.humankinetics.com

United States: Human Kinetics, P.O. Box 5076, Champaign, IL 61825-5076
800-747-4457
e-mail: humank@hkusa.com

Canada: Human Kinetics, 475 Devonshire Road, Unit 100, Windsor, ON N8Y 2L5
800-465-7301 (in Canada only)
e-mail: orders@hkcanada.com

Europe: Human Kinetics, 107 Bradford Road, Stanningly
Leeds LS28 6AT, United Kingdom
+44 (0) 113 255 5665
e-mail: hk@hkeurope.com

Australia: Human Kinetics, 57A Price Avenue, Lower Mitcham, South Australia 5062
08 8277 1555
e-mail: liahka@senet.com.au

New Zealand: Human Kinetics, P.O. Box 105-231, Auckland Central
09-523-3462
e-mail: hkp@ihug.co.nz

Contents

Activity Finder

The activity finder uses five categories to assist the reader in locating appropriate activities quickly.

1. Activity—Name of the cooperative learning activity. Activities marked with an asterisk are best played in a large group; otherwise small groupings are suggested.
2. Chapter and Page Number—Location of the activity in the text.
3. Level—Specific grade level the activity is most appropriate for. Primary (indicated by **P**) includes early preschool through grade 3, while Intermediate (indicated by **I**) includes upper elementary through middle school. Within the activity itself, the suggested level can be found in the upper right corner. Each activity provides several variations in order to better meet the needs of all students.
4. Psychomotor Goal(s)—Psychomotor goals that can be achieved as a result of participation in each activity. The associated cognitive and affective goals appear within the text of each activity.
5. Cooperative Learning Structure—An appropriate goal structure is identified, although several structures are suggested within the text of each activity.

Activity	Chapter/ Page	Level	Psychomotor Goal(s)	Cooperative Learning Structure
Bear on the Loose	5/83	P	Spatial awareness; locomotor skills	Co-op Play
Blowin' Balloons*	6/99	P	Spatial/effort awareness	Co-op Play
Body Parts A' Movin'	4/60	P	Body/spatial awareness	Think-Share-Perform
Body Parts Aerobics	6/102	I	Cardiovascular endurance; muscular strength	Jigsaw Perform
Bump Over	5/86	I	Effort/spatial awareness; manipulative skills	Collective Score
Carousel—A Folk Dance With Two Pairs	6/90	P	Step-draw step	Think-Share-Perform
Challenges	8/120	I	Various components of fitness	Think-Share Perform
Collective Score Exercises	8/118	P I	Muscular strength; cardiovascular endurance	Collective Score
Cooperative Balances	7/111	P I	Static/dynamic balance	Co-op Play
Cooperative Touch and Go	8/122	P I	Cardiovascular endurance; spatial awareness	Collective Score
Cooperative Tumbling Stunts	7/108	P	Body awareness; arm/shoulder strength; flexibility	Co-op Play
Crazy Hoopin' Lines	8/127	I	Flexibility	Co-op Play
Cumberland Square Eight	6/96	I	Dance skills: slide, buzz swing, and star	Pairs-Check-Perform
Cut the Pizza*	4/64	I	Body/spatial/ effort awareness; locomotor skills	Co-op Play

Activity	Chapter/ Page	Level	Psychomotor Goal(s)	Cooperative Learning Structure
Scoop 'Em Up	8/119	P	Cardiovascular endurance	Think-Share-Perform
Shadow Running	8/124	P I	Cardiovascular endurance	Co-op Play
Slalom Blindfold	5/78	I	Body/spatial awareness	Co-op Play
Sneakin' Through the Front Door	4/71	P	Spatial/effort awareness	Co-op Play
Soft Creatures	6/95	P	Body/spatial awareness; dance movements	Co-op Play
Sportball Juggle	5/76	I	Manipulative skills; effort awareness	Pairs-Check-Perform
Student-Created Obstacle Courses	8/125	I	Muscular strength; cardiovascular endurance	Jigsaw Perform
Taketak Tie	5/84	I	Effort awareness	Think-Share-Perform
Telephone Number Dance	6/94	I	Required concepts/skills	Jigsaw Perform
Thunderstorm Dance	6/92	P	Body/spatial awareness	Co-op Co-op Perform
Tinikling	6/98	I	Locomotor skills	Learning Teams
Towel Ball	5/85	I	Manipulative skills; spatial/effort awareness	Co-op Play
21 Frantic Ball	4/67	I	Spatial awareness; manipulative skills	Co-op Play
21 Wall Ball	5/80	I	Manipulative skills; effort awareness	Co-op Play
Under the Rope	4/62	I	Body/spatial awareness	Co-op Play
Wand Grabbing	4/63	P I	Effort awareness	Think-Share-Perform

Preface

Cooperative Learning in Physical Education represents 20 years of personal experiences and thinking in cooperative learning as a public school and university teacher. I have come to believe that many traditional physical education practices and activities are inappropriate for the majority of students. Participation in some competitive activities minimizes motor skill learning and detracts from positive feelings about the self, while individual learning may result in missed opportunities for students to learn from each other. Thus, I have searched for a different way to think about physical education. Terry Orlick's and Alfie Kohn's work helped me to better understand how teaching and learning could be accomplished in a more cooperative way.

In discussions with teachers and teacher education students about cooperative learning in physical education, I have often heard such comments as "Where can I get a copy of those cooperative activities?" "My elementary students would really enjoy these activities!" and "More and more of my middle school students need to learn how to cooperate with others." Another teacher said to me: "I never experienced cooperative learning in school. I wish I would have. I like to see students working together."

I am also concerned about the increasing need for professionals to cooperate in order to solve problems brought about by a perception of strength through individualism and competition and the lack of materials about cooperative learning in physical education. These needs and the concerns of teachers prompted me to write this book.

The potential is great for physical education to become a recognized partner within the general education program. Through a cooperative emphasis, the "whole" student can be engaged in thinking about, learning about, and enjoying movement with peers. In order for this to occur, cooperative learning needs to be more than a unit in games; it needs to be a way of viewing teaching and learning. This "new view" is based on an approach directed at teaching psychomotor goals associated with movement concepts, motor skills, and physical fitness while also achieving affective goals, such as sharing, helping, and caring, and cognitive goals, which include problem solving, creating, and negotiating. We often recognize these affective and cognitive goals as important in physical education, but just as often fail to reach for them in practice.

I regularly teach five physical education classes each week, giving me a chance to observe university students and elementary children. The students respond positively to physical education activities based on cooperation rather than on an individualistic or competitive approach. When questioned about cooperative learning, participants shared statements such as these:

"I didn't know physical education could be this way. The children learned and enjoyed themselves, and I did too!" —Teacher-education student

"I really like playing with my friends. It's fun to always get to play and help."—Third-grade child

Cooperative Learning in Physical Education is for youth workers, day care providers, teachers, and teacher education students concerned about improving physical education and movement programs for children. Physical education should be **inclusive** because all children have the right to acquire skill and enjoy movement through quality programs. This opportunity should not be contingent upon skill level, gender, or luck. Using cooperative learning is an instructional decision teachers can make that leads to quality physical education.

Cooperative Learning in Physical Education helps teachers put cooperation into practice across the physical education curriculum for early childhood, elementary, and middle-school students. It presents a detailed plan and specific activities for using cooperative learning structures and describes cooperative activities designed to promote psychomotor, cognitive, and affective learning goals. These activities span the content areas of movement concepts and motor skills, dance, games, physical fitness, and gymnastics. Through my ongoing teaching opportunities with children, all activities have been field-tested and found to be developmentally appropriate. If I did not create an activity, the originator is identified at the end of the activity text.

Teachers who want "best practices" for students in physical education work to develop quality physical education programs. Teachers move closer to achieving this goal by asking the question "Do the instructional decisions I make increase the likelihood that a maximum number of students will achieve a maximum number of instructional goals?"

Cooperative Learning in Physical Education is unique because it is the only book that applies cooperative learning, through cooperative structures, in a goal-directed manner across the physical education curriculum. Specific features of *Cooperative Learning in Physical Education* include anecdotal narratives from gymnasium observations, interviews with children and teacher education students, and personal reflections about cooperative learning in physical education. The narratives, interviews, and reflections, titled "Insights from the Gym," will be included throughout the text to provide context, examples, and application for the ideas presented. A section titled "A Time to Reflect" at the end of some chapters will allow the reader to refine and extend thoughts generated by the text. Readers are encouraged to choose those questions most appropriate for their individual situations. References used in the text close each chapter.

The Activity Finder on pages viii-xi will enable a teacher or recreation leader to quickly locate activities with appropriate levels, psychomotor goals, and cooperative learning structures. But the activities should not be attempted until the text has been thoroughly read and understood. If the reader tries to use the activities without understanding the principles of cooperative learning—and particularly cooperative learning in physical education—he or she will probably not be able to lead the activities successfully, and the goal of quality physical education may remain elusive.

Introduction: Quality Physical Education for Children

As he walked into the gym, Josh was thinking, "I wonder if I can do it again today?" The strategy of playing in right field and moving to the end of the batting line had kept Josh out of the softball games the last several days. His teacher, Mr. Stillman, had never even noticed. The softball games were like the rest of the stuff they did in class, just play. Josh thought, "I guess if you don't know how to do the skills and know the rules before you come to class, you just don't learn them." Although a fourth-grader, Josh still felt uncomfortable when running, changing direction, and balancing. Something else bothered Josh: "How come the teacher talked and joked with the kids who were good at games but didn't with the ones who were not?"

As usual, the students were told to run three laps, do 10 push-ups and 10 sit-ups and then get ready to pick teams. As Josh jogged slowly, he saw some kids walking and a few running fast. He wondered why they did this every day. The push-ups and sit-ups were a joke. Norm, Abby, Sara, and Kerry could easily do 60 push-ups, while Nan, Ted, Coop, Phil, Barb, Josh, and Steve could barely do eight; some of his classmates could do about 10 of each exercise.

As the teams were being formed, Josh knew he would be picked last for the softball game. He was right. Unsure of how to throw, hit, or run the bases, Josh performed his strategy to perfection. As he slowly moved to the back of the hitting line, he wondered why the teacher never taught him how to throw, hit, or run the bases. Was he the only one who did not know how?

In another school, Ann entered the gym and began her workout. Based on her test results, Ann's personalized program included 10 minutes of self-selected aerobic activity, three sets of five push-ups, and 25 sit-ups. As soon as Ann and her classmates completed the warm-up, they moved to the stations that were set up in the gym. These eight stations provided instruction for practicing skills associated with the game of softball. Each station listed five steps for each specific skill. Ann and her partner were working at the catching ground balls station. First, they practiced catching ground balls that were rolled straight to them, then balls rolled to the left, then right, and lastly balls rolled in either direction. As their skill levels increased, the balls were rolled faster.

Ann felt confident in practicing this skill because she remembered the many times her teacher, Mr. Maring, had them traveling through space in different pathways and levels while playing with balls in all kinds of different situations. She remembered yesterday when he explained how lowering her center of gravity, keeping a wide base of support, and watching the ball would help her catch the ball. It really helped when he showed her what he meant, and then watched her do it to make sure she understood. Another thing that helped her learn was partner checking. All the students would watch their partners, check off on a task card the parts of the skill performed correctly, and then give help on parts that needed extra practice. Using the task cards and partner checking really helped Ann learn; she also liked helping her partner learn. As Ann was leaving physical education class, she thought about how much she had learned. She liked that.

Instructional Goals

In the kindergarten through middle school physical education program, learning is centered on psychomotor, cognitive, and affective goals (Grineski 1993). Major goals from the psychomotor domain include the following:

- Demonstrating efficient body and spatial awareness movement
- Acquiring nonlocomotor, locomotor, manipulative, game/sport, and dance skills
- Attaining healthful levels of physical fitness

Cognitive goals include the following:

- Naming and locating body parts
- Knowing body part actions and relation of body parts to objects in space

- Understanding mechanical principles related to skill performance
- Creating and modifying games and dances
- Applying strategies in sport and game situations

Affective goals include the following:

- Demonstrating positive social interactions with peers
- Cooperating with others to accomplish tasks

Emphasis on these goals results in programs that are goal-directed: Teachers select learning activities to accomplish specific instructional goals. Participation in goal-directed programs is likely to produce skillful, physically fit, knowledgeable, and caring movers (Grineski 1993). Obviously Josh was involved in a program that was not goal-directed; rather, it was game-directed for the motor elite. Ann's program, in contrast, focused on learning. The potential for Ann and her classmates to become skillful, physically fit, knowledgeable, and caring was much higher than for Josh and his peers.

Quality Physical Education

Quality physical education can be defined as students achieving instructional goals as a result of instructional decisions made by the teacher. Increases in quality are related to more students achieving more instructional goals. It is clear that Josh's class was not experiencing quality physical education, while Ann's class was.

A Common Belief System

Teachers working toward the goal of quality physical education share a common belief system. Some of these beliefs include the following:

- Being a physical education teacher is important.
- Physical education is a valuable instructional subject making significant contributions to students.
- Every student has the right to maximal and productive learning; opportunities for learning are not contingent upon skill, luck, gender, power, or aggression.
- Physical education and athletics have separate goals.
- Teachers can affect student performance positively through a clear understanding of teaching and learning.

In addition, these teachers demonstrate a passion for their work; they seek new information about students, pedagogy, and physical education; and they are interested in talking about what students learn and what they as teachers learn from students. Teachers striving for quality physical education look through a "lens" that focuses on the question, "What can I do so more students learn more?"

Quality Physical Education and Best Practices

Even with these beliefs in place, instructional decision making is difficult and challenging. Teachers must continually ask themselves, "What practices will result in more students achieving a greater number of instructional goals?" Some practices currently advocated as being effective include the following:

- Outcome-based education
- Developmentally and pedagogically appropriate principles
- Skill-theme curricula
- Holistic physical fitness approach
- Reduced competition
- Research-driven teaching skills
- Cooperative learning

When teachers use cooperative learning, quality physical education will likely increase. The major reason for this increase is the inclusive, rather than exclusive, nature of cooperative learning: All students work together, with each student's contribution needed for goal achievement.

For example, in the cooperative physical fitness activity "Help Me Up Sit-Ups," students lie on the floor, with the knees bent, while holding a parachute on their waist. On command, all perform sit-ups by pulling on the parachute and sitting up. The pulling action helps up not only the individual student but also the student located on the opposite side of the parachute.

The next three chapters describe cooperative learning, relate cooperative learning to physical education, and detail a plan for using cooperative learning in physical education.

Summary

The purpose of physical education is students achieving instructional goals from the psychomotor, cognitive, and affective domains of learning. Quality physical education is defined as students achieving goals because of the instructional decisions made by the teacher. Quality increases when more students achieve more instructional goals.

Instructional decision making is related to what is considered best practice in physical education. Cooperative learning is a best practice that results in many students achieving a number of psychomotor, cognitive, and affective goals.

A Time to Reflect

1. Do you know anyone who experienced physical education situations similar to Josh's or Ann's? Did you? As a physical educator, what is your response?

2. What do you believe is the purpose of physical education? Ask a number of people this question. Do you agree or disagree with their responses? Was there variety in the responses? If so, how do you account for it? If you said learning is the purpose of physical education, do you have real proof that learning occurs? Ask students of different ages and ask adults what they learned in physical education. If they cannot remember, ask if they can remember what they learned in reading and math classes. If they can remember what they learned in these subjects, why can't they remember what they learned in physical education?

3. Do you think quality is part of most physical education programs? If you answered "yes," why do you feel that way? If you answered "no," what are the obstacles? Ask other physical educators the same question. Ask teachers of other subjects whether they think trying to get more students to achieve more instructional goals in their subject area is reasonable. Think about the responses from all these different teachers. What do they mean?

4. When you teach, what practices do you or will you use to work toward quality physical education? Why did you select these practices? Where did you learn them?

5. Think about the effect teachers have on their students. How do you want your students to describe you after they leave your program? What do you think parents, teachers, and principals will say about your program? What will your response be to these comments?

6. What is your prior experience with cooperative learning? Do you personally like to learn alone, together with, or against others? Most learning in school, kindergarten through college level, is individual or competitive. Will you only teach in ways that you were taught? Will you only teach in ways you enjoy learning or will you teach in ways that allow for the differences among your students?

CHAPTER 1

Goal Structures, Learning, and Physical Education

Goal structure can be defined as the way students physically and verbally interact with peers and/or teachers when engaged in learning (Johnson and Johnson 1975). Another way to think about goal structure is to view it as a type of interdependence among students while they are learning. This interdependence can be positive, negative, or non-interdependent.

Goal Structures: Competitive, Individual, and Cooperative

To maximize learning, the physical education teacher needs to determine which goal structure(s) will result in goal achievement for the greatest number of students (Grineski 1993a). Good decisions about goal structures lead directly to quality physical education as described in the introduction. Although selecting appropriate goal structures is one of the most critical decisions teachers make, it is the one they are most likely to overlook (Johnson and Johnson 1975).

Three different goal structures can be used for goal achievement. They are competitive, individual, and cooperative.

Competitive Goal Structure: Definition, Examples, and Description

Students work against other students in attempting to achieve a goal that can only be achieved by one student or group of students. Goal achievement is mutually exclusive.

Group contests and tournaments are two examples of physical education activities with competitive goal structures. These activities can be categorized as "zero sum" with one winner and one loser or "negative sum" with one winner and many losers. Another category is contingency activities. In contingency activities, continued participation depends on uninterrupted success in that activity (Brown and Grineski 1992). For example, the teacher tells students to sit down upon missing in a rope skipping contest.

During competitively structured learning, students are negatively interdependent upon each other (Deutsch 1949). Negative interdependence occurs when one student's or group of students' goal achievement is linked with another student's or group of students' *not achieving* their goals. This type of interdependence is evident when students compete to determine who can skip rope the most times. One student can do the most only when all of the other students do less. Striving to achieve the goal blocks other students from achieving the goal: Goal achievement is mutually exclusive.

Although competitive activities continue to dominate the K–12 physical education curriculum, competition and its relationship to learning in physical education has never been examined. In spite of this research void, in a survey of 500 elementary education and physical education majors, students reported that over 90% of their physical education experiences were competitive. In a review of 288 games in five different elementary physical education textbooks, the author found that over 90% of the games were competitive (Grineski 1991a).

When K–8 physical education teachers were asked which activities occupied the greatest amount of time in their programs, they reported that competitive games dominated (Ross et al. 1985; Ross et al. 1987). Their programs heavily emphasized soccer, basketball, kickball, dodgeball, and relays.

Competitive activities have been used in physical education for decades. For example, Bancroft's 1928 edition of *Games for the Playground, Home, School and Gymnasium* recommended many competitive games and activities. There was even a version of the competitive game dodgeball called "Elizabethan Dodge" played in seventeenth-century England (Grineski and Brown 1995).

Several positive outcomes are usually believed to be associated with competition in physical education. The major assumption underlying these associations is that human beings have an inbred predisposition for competition and, therefore, must compete to be successful in a competitive world. Competition is generally associated with the following outcomes:

- Character development
- Enhancement of self-esteem and self-confidence
- Motivation to achieve
- Establishment of excellence as a goal
- Maintenance of interest for participants
- Sense of personal achievement through out-performing others (Brown and Grineski 1992)
- Fair set of rewards and punishments for outcomes associated with the competitive activity (Kohn 1994; Greendorfer 1987; Johnson and Johnson 1975)

Alternative ways of thinking about competition and its effect on learning emerge when different assumptions and outcomes are examined. Interestingly enough, many daily interactions are cooperative, not competitive, for we often depend on the contributions of others. In addition, competition, with its reliance on standards (e.g. rules, equipment), produces a less than desirable situation for most children, because children are not "standard." Rather, they are heterogeneous across many variables: ability, interest, experiences, and maturity. In other words, the individual differences of children are not aligned with the requirements needed for competition. As a result, competition can be an experience that inhibits learning for many children. Moreover, because of the high failure rate associated with competition, only those who have opportunities for success are motivated (Brown and Grineski 1992). Competition may be appropriate for a select group within a class who exhibit similar skill levels and physical fitness competence and who choose to compare performances with peers (Grineski 1993a). Several studies, however, have demonstrated that competitive activities limit learning opportunities (Grineski 1993b):

- 75% of ball contacts were made by 40% of the players during a third-grade soccer game (Grineski 1990).
- 35% of players never caught the ball, while 52% of players never threw the ball during a fifth-grade kickball game (Wilson 1976).
- Three students never touched the ball nor ran the length of the gym floor during a fifth-grade sideline soccer game (Grineski 1991d).
- 20 third-grade children participating in a one-hour softball game had a total of 39 throwing and catching opportunities. The average number of throwing and catching opportunities for each child for the one-hour game was 2.3 (Grineski 1992).
- Children participating in an hour-long hockey game had possession of the puck less than two minutes each (Robbins 1979).

As suggested by these observations, participation in traditional competitive activities may not provide all children opportunities to practice, acquire, and refine skills necessary for successful participation. Using competitive physical education activities can be detrimental to students when learning is the desired outcome (Brown and Grineski 1992).

INSIGHTS FROM THE GYM

The negative impact associated with competition is illustrated by this preservice teacher education student's memories of physical education: "I hated physical education. I worried every day when I came to the gym, what would happen today? I always felt I was on the spot, with everybody judging and watching me. Nobody seemed to care."

Individual Goal Structure: Definition, Examples, and Description

Students work alone without peer interaction in trying to achieve a goal. Goal achievement is not dependent upon other students' efforts at goal achievement.

Individualized contract programs for gymnastics and physical fitness training, country line dancing, rope skipping routines, and aerobic dancing are examples of physical education activities based on an individual goal structure.

During individual learning, students are non-interdependent upon each other for learning (Deutsch 1949). Non-interdependence is defined as no working relationship existing between individuals during goal achievement. During individual learning, one student's goal achievement or lack of goal achievement does not influence others' goal achievement or lack of goal achievement. Non-interdependence can be observed when individual students are attempting to perform as many push-ups as possible in 30 seconds. Student achievement has nothing to do with others achieving or not achieving the goal. Students work alone; interaction is not necessary, required, or positively reinforced.

Individual learning in physical education has an historical context. Early programs emphasized personal training in gymnastics, calisthenics, track and field, and ball skills. Movement education programming grounded in the movement theories of Rudolf Laban (1963) continued the emphasis of individual learning. Locke's (1976) analysis of individualization in physical education is the major work in this area. The Prudential Fitnessgram Program (1994) is an example of a physical fitness test and activity component using an individual approach.

The lack of interaction is noticeable as individual students do push-ups.

A belief that superior effort and productivity result from individual learning in physical education is widely accepted. The following outcomes are generally believed to be associated with individual learning:

- Learning can be personalized for every student.
- Less teacher time is required.
- Individual learning will enhance goal achievement.
- All students experience success.
- Individual learning eliminates social problems.
- Personal identity and character is developed through working alone.
- Individual learning eliminates discipline problems.

Individual learning, although appropriate under some conditions, usually does not achieve most of these outcomes for most students. Given the number of students that teachers must plan for, teach, and evaluate, finding the necessary time to truly personalize instruction for each student may be impossible.

Individual learning does not promote positive interpersonal interaction among students because students are not required and are usually forbidden to interact with each other. Social problems are not eliminated when students are isolated from peers, because stereotyping, labeling, and bigotry may flourish.

Effective discipline may also require ingredients that extend beyond the individual, such as peer conflict resolution. Personal identity and character building do not result so much from working alone as from experiencing positive interactions with others. Interestingly, because quality learning is thought of in terms of the whole child, success is generally defined as achievement across the cognitive, psychomotor, and affective areas. Although learning alone does not deliver on affective goals, it is useful for some psychomotor and cognitive skill practice.

Cooperative Goal Structure: Definition, Examples, and Description

> *Students work together to achieve a goal. All students must make a contribution to goal achievement and are held accountable for their contributions. Goal achievement is mutually inclusive.*

An example of physical education activities using a cooperative goal structure is collective score activities, where all scores or performances are added together for a group total. When teachers cooperatively structure learning, positive interdependence develops among participants. Students understanding that they can only attain the goal if other students attain the goal is the definition of positive interdependence (Deutsch 1962). A sense of being on the "same side" is the result of this goal structure.

Another example of positive interdependence in a cooperatively structured physical education activity is small group pyramid play. When a teacher presents the goal of building a five-person pyramid so all are involved in balancing or supporting, students are positively interdependent because each student must contribute with balance or support to the building pyramid or else they do not achieve the goal. Many times while teaching cooperative physical education activities, I have observed the following behaviors: kindness, caring, helping, teaching, cheering, and listening. We should expect these benefits for our students through participation in physical education.

The Effects of Competitive, Individual, and Cooperative Goal Structures on Learning: What We Know

The belief that cooperative learning structures are superior to competitive and individual is based on scientific, not just anecdotal, evidence.

The Effects on Learning in General

The effects the three different goal structures have on learning have been studied extensively outside the field of physical education. A comprehensive analysis of 122 studies examined the three goal structures and their effects on achievement (Johnson et al. 1981). The conclusion was that cooperative learning is associated with higher achievement than either individual or competitive learning. These findings were similar for all age groups, in all subject areas, and across all examined tasks.

In two additional studies, Johnson, Johnson, and Maruyama (1983), and Johnson and Johnson (1983) examined the effects of goal structures on social and affective development. These studies revealed cooperative learning to be superior to individual and competitive learning in the following areas:

- Attitudes toward school
- Working-together skills
- Sense of self-esteem
- Emotional maturity
- Social skills
- Feelings of acceptance
- Affinity for other students and school personnel
- Realistic view of self
- Interpersonal attraction
- Concern for others

Several studies support cooperative rather than individual or competitive learning in promoting positive attitudes and interactions among persons with and without disabilities (Johnson and Johnson 1984; Grineski 1989b) and among persons of different races and socioeconomic status (Alport 1954; Sherif and Sherif 1956; Slavin 1990).

The Effects on Learning in Physical Education

Within the field of physical education ample evidence shows that physical education goals may be achieved better through cooperative goal structures than through individual or competitive goal structures. One study examined the effect that individual, competitive, and cooperative goal structured physical education activities had on four measures of physical fitness and social interactions for second- and third-grade children (Grineski 1993a). This study revealed that students participating in the cooperative group demonstrated more improvement in physical fitness and exhibited higher levels of positive social interactions than students in the individual and competitive groups. The effects games had on the positive social behavior interactions of kindergarten children was also studied. The major conclusion was that cooperative games resulted in more positive social behaviors than did competitive games (Grineski 1989a). In a related study conducted with four-year-old children with and without disabilities, cooperative games were associated with a higher incidence of positive social behaviors and a lower incidence of negative behaviors than a program of individual physical education activities (Grineski 1989b). In another study, cooperative physical education activities resulted in more positive social interactions than did activities that were individually structured for 8- to 12-year-old children with emotional and behavioral disorders (Grineski 1993c).

Working together to achieve a common goal encourages positive social interaction.

Orlick's (1978, 1981a, 1981b, 1982) work has provided additional evidence linking positive benefits and participation in cooperative games. Yoder (1993) reported that using cooperative learning in dance can enhance group work, social interactions, and learning for all students.

These findings are consistent with those generated by Johnson, Maruyama, Johnson, Nelson, and Skon (1981); Johnson and Johnson (1983); and Johnson, Johnson, and Maruyama (1983): Cooperative learning is superior to individual and competitive learning in the areas of achievement, group relations, and social development.

Although cooperative learning has not yet gained wide acceptance in physical education, it has much to offer teachers concerned about promoting goal achievement for as many students as possible in a quality physical education program. This has been demonstrated in the previously described studies for students with and without disabilities, across various age levels, and in the content areas of games, physical fitness, dance, gymnastics, and motor skill acquisition. Cooperative learning *works* in physical education; it is an inclusive practice that encourages and supports learning because all students are required to work together, with each student's contribution needed for goal achievement.

Cooperative learning in physical education is beneficial to students when the goal is to encourage and maintain positive social interaction. Some of the behaviors promoted by cooperative learning include trust, affinity for others, acceptance, helping, sharing, working together, reducing bias, and positive attitudes. For example, "Under the Rope" (Grineski 1991c) is a problem solving activity designed to achieve the goals of encouraging and maintaining positive social interaction and enhancing body and spatial awareness. This activity requires small groups of students, without using their hands, to pass under a rope that is being held by fellow players who also cannot use their hands. Players switch positions and then share workable ideas.

INSIGHTS FROM THE GYM

Following instruction in the "Under the Rope" activity, a group of third-graders looked at their teacher with bewilderment and asked "How do we do this?" while one student said, "We can do it." After five minutes of talking, helping, and moving, the group shouted, "We did it!"

Cooperative learning can enhance self-esteem as a result of each student's contribution to goal achievement being directed at and needed for goal achievement. "Collective Score Push-Ups" is a fitness activity designed to enhance self-esteem and promote arm and shoulder strength. It can also be used for practicing the skills of counting, adding, and remembering. Students in small groups do as many push-ups as possible in a given time and add their scores for a collective total, trying to achieve a predetermined total (Grineski 1994).

I have repeatedly witnessed students' smiles of satisfaction and shouts of enjoyment when they realized that their number of completed push-ups, when added together with their teammates', resulted in achieving the goal of 150 class push-ups. Cooperative learning can also be used to help students achieve goals such as critical thinking, creativity, perspective taking (i.e., understanding another's way of thinking), and negotiation. Student-designed games, dances, and obstacle courses are examples of activities that can be used to achieve these goals. The collaborative problem solving associated with cooperative learning provides an appropriate means not only for achieving cognitive goals but also for attaining psychomotor and affective outcomes associated with student-designed activities.

A wonderful creative dance activity that meets the needs of the "whole" child is the "Thunderstorm Dance" (Grineski 1991b). To teach it, begin with a discussion about the characteristics of a thunderstorm—wind, rain, lightning, thunder, hail, and clouds. Assign small groups of students to each thunderstorm part. Provide props (e.g., Frisbee for wind) and allow each small group time to develop and practice their thunderstorm part. Then connect the parts together, practicing in sections, until the dance is complete. The theme of the dance can be changed to match season or grade-level interest.

Elbow swings can be 'tornadoes' during the Thunderstorm Dance.

In addition to the affective and cognitive goals that can be enhanced through cooperative learning, many psychomotor goals can be achieved. As a result of the encouragement, reinforcement, and teaching that is carried out by peers during cooperative learning, the goals of movement concept understanding, skill acquisition, and physical fitness competence can be achieved. Examples of peer teaching include use of partner checking cards, small group learning teams, and participation in activities like "Shadow Running" (Grineski 1994). This activity requires students, in pairs standing one in front of the other, to attempt to run through the playspace for a specific amount of time while maintaining an arms'-length distance between them.

This activity not only enhances psychomotor skills; it also helps students understand movement concepts like pathways, general and self-space, direction, speed, and levels (i.e., high, medium, and low planes). Both "Shadow Running" and "Thunderstorm Dance" achieve the affective goals of partner helping and wanting your partner to be successful and safe.

The above descriptions of "Under the Rope," "Collective Score Push-Ups," "Thunderstorm Dance," and "Shadow Running" suggest that when physical educators use cooperative learning, students maximize their goal achievements in all domains: psychomotor, cognitive, and affective. Moreover, cooperative physical education results in teaching and learning that is goal-directed, so that the potential for quality physical education increases.

Summary

Goal structure is defined as the ways students interact or do not interact during goal achievement. This interaction can be understood in terms of interdependence among students while learning. In competitive learning, students experience a negative interdependence with achievement linked to others' non-achievement; in cooperative learning, students experience positive interdependence, with achievement linked to others' achievement. Non-interdependence is associated with individual learning, with students not required to interact during goal achievement. Cooperative learning is superior to both competitive and individual learning across measures of physical achievement, social and affective development, and multigroup relations.

A Time to Reflect

1. Why do you think the idea of goal structure is not accepted in physical education as it is in other subject areas? Is using goal structure contingent upon having instructional goals? Placek's (1983) landmark study of perception of successful teaching in physical education suggests that many teachers do not focus on learning through instructional goals but on keeping students busy, happy, and good. Is there a relationship between having goals and using goal structures? Think of all the reasons why goal structure is not part of many physical education teachers' decision-making processes. How will this thinking influence your development as a teacher?

2. What causes so many physical education teachers to overuse individual and competitive learning, while ignoring cooperative learning? Think about your life history as a student and athlete. Think about how adults and peers reinforced your accomplishments. Remember past physical education teachers. What influence did their programs and teaching have on you? Remember past coaches. What influence did their programs and coaching

have on you? Think carefully about how physical educators have been socialized.

3. Do you believe that human beings are born competitors? Do you think that school programs should prepare children for a competitive world? Is motivation and excellence exclusively associated with competition? Were you generally successful in physical education competitions? Think about the students who were not. How would they answer these same questions? If differently, what accounts for that difference? Think about all the actions and interactions you had today. How many were competitive? How many relied on other people's contributions?

4. Take some time to observe students participating in physical education activities. How many different students had opportunities to practice motor skills and good sport skills, and to be engaged in using the rules, directions, and strategies associated with the activity? If opportunities for learning and practicing were maximal for a few and minimal for many, why do you think this occurred? Do you have any ideas of how to change any part of the activity to provide more learning and practicing for more students?

5. Do you think that cooperative learning can work in physical education? What are reasons some might think it will not work? What are reasons others might give for cooperative learning working in physical education? What is your opinion? Why do you think this way?

References

Alport, G. 1954. *The nature of prejudice.* New York: Addison-Wesley.

Bancroft, J. 1928. *Games for the playground, home, school, and gymnasium.* New York: Macmillan.

Brown, L., and S. Grineski. 1992. Competition in physical education: An educational contradiction? *Journal of Physical Education, Recreation and Dance* 63(1): 17-19 and 77.

Deutsch, M. 1949. An experimental study of the effects of co-operation and competition upon group process. *Human Relations* 2: 199-233.

———. 1962. Cooperation and trust: Some theoretical notes. In *Nebraska Symposium of Motivation*, edited by M.R. Jones, 275-319. Lincoln, NE: University of Nebraska Press.

Greendorfer, S. 1987. Psycho-social correlates of organized physical activity. *Journal of Physical Education, Recreation and Dance* 58(7): 59-62.

Grineski, S. 1989a. Children, games, and prosocial behavior: Insight and connections. *Journal of Physical Education, Recreation and Dance* 60(8): 20-25.

———. 1989b. *Effects of cooperative games on the prosocial behavior interactions
of young children with and without impairments.* Unpublished Ph.D. dis-
sertation, University of North Dakota.

———. 1990. [Practice trials: Third-grade soccer game]. Unpublished raw data.

———. 1991a. Affective learning in physical education. *Teaching Elementary Physical Education* 2(6): 9.

———. 1991b. Creative dance: A curriculum priority. *Teaching Elementary
Physical Education* 2(2): 11-13.

———. 1991c. Promoting success in physical education: Cooperatively
structured learning. *PALAESTRA* 7(2): 26-29.

———. 1991d. [Practice trials: Fifth-grade soccer game]. Unpublished raw
data.

———. 1992. [Practice trials: Third-grade softball game]. Unpublished raw
data.

———. 1993a. Achieving educational goals in physical education: A missing
ingredient. *Journal of Physical Education, Recreation and Dance* 64(5): 32-34.

———. 1993b. Children, cooperative learning, and physical education.
Teaching Elementary Physical Education 4(6): 10-11 and 14.

———. 1993c. [Interactions and physical education: Students with behavior disorders]. Unpublished raw data.

———. 1994. Cooperative fitness activities. *Teaching Elementary Physical Education* 5(1): 14-15.

Grineski, S., and L. Brown. 1995. Dodgeball: When will the game end? *Teaching Middle School Physical Education* 1(1): 6, 7-15.

Johnson, D., and R. Johnson. 1975. *Learning together and alone.* Englewood
Cliffs, NJ: Prentice-Hall.

———. 1983. Social interdependence and perceived academic and personal
support in the classroom. *Journal of Social Psychology* 120: 77-82.

———. 1984. Building acceptance of differences between handicapped and
nonhandicapped students: The effects of cooperative and individualistic problems. *Journal of Social Psychology* 122: 257-267.

Johnson D., R. Johnson, and G. Maruyama. 1983. Interdependence and interpersonal attraction among heterogeneous and homogeneous individuals: A theoretical formulation and meta-analysis of the research.
Review of Educational Research 53: 5-54.

Johnson, D., G. Maruyama, R. Johnson, D. Nelson, and L. Skon. 1981. The
effects of cooperative, competitive and individualistic goal structures
on achievement: A meta-analysis. *Psychological Bulletin* 89: 47-62.

Kohn, A. 1994. (2nd ed.). *No contest.* Boston: Houghton Mifflin.

Laban, R. (1963). Modern Educational Dance. London: Macdonald and
Evans.

Locke, L. 1976. Personalized learning in physical education. *Journal of Physical Education and Recreation* 47(6): 5-32.

Orlick, T. 1978. *The cooperative sports and games book*. New York: Pantheon.

———. 1981a. Cooperative play socialization among preschool children. *Journal of Individual Psychology* 37: 54-67.

———. 1981b. Positive socialization via cooperative games. *Developmental Psychology* 4: 426-429.

———. 1982. *The second cooperative sports and games book*. New York: Pantheon.

Placek, J. 1983. Conceptions of success in teaching: Busy, happy, and good? In *Teaching in physical education*, edited by T. Templin and J. Olson, 46-55. Champaign, IL: Human Kinetics.

The Prudential Fitnessgram. 1994. 1230 Preston Road, Dallas, TX, 75230.

Robbins, S. 1979. Different strokes for smaller folks. *Canadian American Association for Health, Physical Education, Recreation and Dance* 56(May/June): 73-76.

Ross, J., C. Dotson, G. Gilbert, and S. Katz. 1985. The national children and youth fitness study I. What are kids doing in school physical education? *Journal of Physical Education, Recreation and Dance* 56(10): 73-76.

Ross, J., R. Pate, C. Corbin, L. Delpy, and R. Gold. 1987. The national children and youth fitness study II. What is going on in the physical education program? *Journal of Physical Education, Recreation and Dance* 58(9): 78-84.

Sherif, M. and M. Sherif. 1956. Experiments in group conflict. *Scientific American* 195(32): 54-58.

Slavin, R. 1990. *Cooperative learning: Theory, research and practice*. Englewood Cliffs, NJ: Prentice-Hall.

Wilson, N. 1976. The frequency and patterns of selected motor skills by third grade and fourth grade boys and girls in the game of kickball. In *Children Moving*, edited by G. Graham, S. Holt-Hale, and M. Parker, 468. Mountain View, CA: Mayfield.

Yoder, L. 1993. Cooperative learning and dance education. *Journal of Physical Education, Recreation and Dance* 64(5): 47-51 and 56.

CHAPTER 2

Cooperative Learning in Physical Education

Students come to physical education with various needs and expectations. They want to move and have fun, learn new skills, express themselves, be members of a group, and feel competent and successful. Teachers of physical education, based on past experiences, professional preparation, interest, and commitment come to physical education with a mission (i.e., what is physical education and its purpose) and a vision (i.e., what it can be) for students. Some teachers provide mostly large group competitive activities with minimal emphasis on skill acquisition. Such teachers often believe that physical education's purpose is to provide fun, not skill development; or they may not be interested in teaching physical education due to a commitment to coaching.

INSIGHTS FROM THE GYM

When university students were asked to identify what they thought was most important to their physical education teachers, this is how they replied:

"I think we were."

"I am not sure—I know it wasn't the students."

"Coaching. That's how he spent his time during our PE class. Getting ready for coaching."

"I don't remember being taught skills."

These perceptions parallel findings of Kneer (1994), Seagrave (1987), and Chu (1980). These researchers found that teachers don't include skill acquisition or fitness competence as part of a grade; teachers prefer coaching to teaching, and spend more preparation time with coaching plans than teaching plans. Many physical education teachers spend 1 hour of preparation in physical education to 12 hours of preparation for coaching (Chu 1980).

Some physical educators, however, teach so that many students successfully achieve a variety of psychomotor, cognitive, and affective goals. Their aim is quality physical education for all students. Several professional documents support this type of curriculum delivery. These include: NASPE's (1992) "The Physically Educated Person," NASPE's (1992) *Developmentally Appropriate Physical Education Practices for Children: A Position Statement of the National Association for Sport and Physical Education/Developed by the Council on Physical Education for Children,* and NASPE's (1995) *Moving Into the Future: National Standards for Physical Education: A Guide to Content and Assessment.* In addition, teachers who do work toward quality programs typically use multiple teaching styles, goal-directed curricula, and appropriate assessment strategies. These characteristics reinforce a commitment to student learning through an ongoing concern for improving the practices of planning, teaching, and evaluating.

INSIGHTS FROM THE GYM

When teacher education students were asked to describe their histories in physical education, many of physical education's problems came to life:

"My PE classes never allowed time to learn skills. We seemed to do stuff . . . competitive and elimination games."

"Although I was highly skilled, many of the other students were not. . . . I did not have much fun because these students did not present much of a challenge."

"The problem was receiving instructor feedback: We received none."

"There was never any explanation of skills. Basically, if you didn't know it you were not going to learn it in gym."

"I do not think I will ever forget this game we played. There were two teams and each team had two balls. We also had three pins and it was our job to protect the pins from being hit down. I always got so scared and hoped that I'd be hit by the ball right away so I'd be out of the game."

Rationale: Why Change?

In the early 1990s, some leaders in physical education began to warn professionals about the future of the field (Colby, Steir, and Jensen 1994). They said that physical education must change or risk elimination. One message coming from this movement was strong and clear: Unless teaching in physical education focuses on students and their learning, physical education as we know it will be non-existent within 20 years. This is a hard message to swallow, as we know; the image and reputation of physical education has been, and continues to be, troubled (Grineski 1994).

The reputation and image of physical education can be changed. The profession's vision should be quality physical education programs for all students. The mission should be planning, teaching, and evaluating physical education so it makes valuable contributions to the lives of all students. This "overhaul" will require a new way of thinking about physical education: Student learning must be linked to instructional decisions made by the teacher. Cooperative learning is an instructional decision that applies ideas related to student learning across the psychomotor, cognitive, and affective domains. Why change? If we don't we may lose the only school subject that impacts the whole child through the medium of movement: physical education.

Necessary Ingredients for Cooperative Learning

Teachers using cooperative learning design small-group learning activities based on student interaction. In order for this learning to be maximized, four ingredients are necessary:

1. Forming teams
2. Positive interdependence
3. Individual accountability
4. Collaborative skills

Forming Teams

In order to gain benefits associated with cooperative learning, the task of forming teams should be thoughtfully undertaken. Groups should be heterogeneous in gender, race, economic status, and ability. Improvement in thinking skills, greater frequency of giving and receiving assistance, and broader ranges of perspective occur when groups are mixed (Johnson et al. 1984). When beginning to use cooperative learning, start with pairs, if possible. Pairs allow for maximum participation, increased communication, and opportunity to practice necessary collaborative skills. Pairs grouping transitions easily to larger groups of four or six, thereby minimizing management time. Students can be assigned to cooperative groups by the teacher or groups can be randomly assigned. Teacher selected groups usually result in effective groupings and take less time to organize. A method for randomly forming groups is to ask students to find a peer who can answer a question, such as, "Find someone who had toast for breakfast." Another method is to ask students to find peers they have not been with during the week.

Positive Interdependence

At the heart of cooperative learning is positive interdependence. Positive interdependence occurs when learning requires the goal achievement of one student to be connected to the goal achievement of another. Goal achievement in cooperative learning is mutually inclusive—a joint, rather than individual, effort. Simply put, "I need you and you need me to achieve our goal."

The activity "Partner Cards" requires pairs of students to select a card that is face down in the center of the gym, read the card, and then together perform the task or answer the question that is written on the card. Students are positively interdependent because the cards are written in such a way that it is impossible for one student to answer the question without his or her partner's help; two students' contributions are needed for goal achievement. For example, a task card reading "Do 150 push-ups" could be used in the primary grades. Teachers can and should extend or modify challenges to meet the needs of all students.

How many times can you and your partner cooperatively spin the hoop?

INSIGHTS FROM THE GYM

The following observations were made of second-grade children during the "Partner Cards" activity.

"How are we going to do this?"

"I got an idea! Let's each do some and when we get tired, then the other person can do some. OK?"

"OK!"

"Boy you are really good at doing this."

"Thanks."

"This is really fun. Let's see how many cards we can do."

Two third-graders enjoy solving a cooperative movement task.

Positive interdependence takes place through task and reward structuring (Kagan 1992). Task structure defines how students work together during cooperative learning. Physical education tasks can be structured in several ways to yield positive interdependence, including the following:

Small groups produce a single product.

Example: The class is divided into groups of four. Each group creates a dance that is based on a theme, then shares their theme dance with the other groups.

Labor is divided within student learning teams.

Example: In groups of four, and following teacher explanation and demonstration about the layup, members of each student learning team are assigned a job for layup skill practice.

- Student One performs layup.
- Student Two observes to see if parts of skill are performed correctly (Step-Hop-Push) and provides feedback.
- Student Three checks correctly performed parts of skill on task card.
- Student Four returns ball to next shooter.

All students achieve a specified level of competence before group progresses to next task.

Example: In groups of four, and learning a sequence of six progressive tinikling steps, students help each other learn so the group can progress to the next tinikling step. *Tinikling* is a small group dance with two dancers moving eight-foot poles together and apart, while dancers step sometimes between, and sometimes outside of, the poles.

Students collaborate to achieve a group goal.

Example: During the large group game of "Fish Gobbler" (Orlick 1978), students must perform the required motor, cognitive, and affective skills in order to successfully achieve the group goal. Group goals take the form of commands given by the Fish Gobbler (e.g., "Fishnet"—all join hands, "Sardines"—all lie close together, "Clam"—all lie next to each other and perform v-sits).

Positive interdependence can also be achieved through reward structuring (e.g., receiving stickers for goal achievement). Here are two examples:

A group is rewarded for achieving a predetermined group or class total score (e.g., 30 children performed 300 push-ups) when participating in the fitness activity "Collective Score Push-Ups."

A group is rewarded for achieving a predetermined average group or class performance score (e.g., 30 children average length of standing long jump skill is 40 inches) when performing the standing long jump.

Strong positive interdependence requires these four conditions:

1. Face to face positive verbal interactions
2. Positive physical interaction when appropriate
3. Maximum contribution by group members
4. Success of each group member contingent upon success of other group members

In Group Juggle, wanting your teammates to be successful and watching the ball usually result in success.

For example, in the "Partner Cards" activity, both students work closely together, encourage each other, and must actively participate in order to accomplish the task. One student cannot be successful alone; positive interdependence is strong.

The next important ingredient needed for effective cooperative learning is individual accountability.

Individual Accountability

Accountability is always important in teaching and learning situations. In cooperative learning it is essential because student learning is the desired result of participation in cooperative learning. The following are three strategies that can be used to hold individuals accountable for both learning and helping others to learn in physical education:

1. The teacher asks students at random for explanations.

   Example: While small groups of students are involved in designing a portion of an obstacle course, the teacher asks an individual student why a piece of equipment was selected and what skill will be practiced by using this equipment.

   The teacher could also ask a student to demonstrate the skill.

Students, in small groups, move through an obstacle course designed by their class.

2. Students share directions and/or strategies.

Example: After the class is placed into small groups and practices a mini-game intended to promote a sport skill, each group teaches its game, explaining directions and strategies, to other groups. Each student can be responsible for teaching a specific component of the game.

3. Teachers organize activities to make sure that all are needed.

Example: In the activity "Partner Bouncing," each person has to lift a leg and hold his or her partner's lifted leg while the partner hops in order to be successful.

If teachers think carefully about forming teams, plan for strong positive interdependence, and make sure that all students are held accountable, cooperative learning will be more effective. Unless teachers check to see that students possess and use appropriate collaborative skills, however, maximum gains cannot be achieved.

Collaborative Skills

The collaborative skills needed for cooperative learning include

- listening to others,
- resolving conflict,
- supporting and encouraging others,
- taking turns,
- expressing enjoyment in the success of others, and
- demonstrating the ability to criticize ideas, not individuals (Johnson et al. 1984).

It is very important to teach explicitly the collaborative skills required for a particular activity. Teaching should include clear verbal statements, precise modeling, and checking for understanding through questioning or asking for student examples. For example, a teacher may say, "Jose, that was great how you helped Marsha balance on one foot. Let me show the entire class how you held her hand. Bill, what should be done to maintain our partner's balancing?" In addition, teachers should use and reinforce cooperative vocabulary. Examples include statements like, "We need your help" and "Thanks for helping" and "You worked really hard at helping the group" and "Way to go!" Another effective way to teach collaborative skills is through processing at the end of the lesson. During closure, the teacher asks questions such as, "Do you think we made it so everybody could participate today?" or "What could we do next time to work together better?" and "What words of encouragement did you hear today that made you or others work harder and feel good?"

Since the purpose of cooperative learning is promoting quality physical education and getting along with others, the teaching of collaborative skills is critical. This aspect of cooperative learning is not just important for learning in physical education; it is also vital to the success of those many students who come to school without appropriate social skills. Because getting along with coworkers is a significant job skill, it is important that the learning of these important life skills in schools not be relegated to the "hidden curriculum." In a recent comprehensive analysis of 11,000 findings from studies examining why some students are successful in school, the major conclusion was that positive social interaction greatly influences successful school participation and achievement (Wang, Haaertel, and Walberg 1994). When the four ingredients of cooperative

Working together is enjoyable and challenging.

learning are applied through specific cooperative learning strategies, student interaction during learning can be effectively organized and children gain both physical proficiency and skills that impact their success across the physical education curriculum.

INSIGHTS FROM THE GYM

A game of "Fish Gobbler" (Orlick 1978) illustrates how collaborative skills help children accomplish a goal.

Upon hearing the Fish Gobbler command "Fishnet," most of the children quickly ran to the middle of the playspace and joined hands. The circle formed rapidly, as hands were being held and arms pulled. One boy remained standing about five feet from the circle until one of the other players called, "Over here, c'mon, we need you." When this boy heard the call, he smiled, said, "OK," and joined the circle.

Cooperative Learning Structures

In order for physical education teachers to use cooperative learning effectively, they need to understand and put into practice cooperative learning structures. Structures are methods of arranging students for systematic interaction during cooperative learning; they are content free and serve as building blocks for lessons. Unless teachers understand and use structures, they are limited to teaching through the "activities" approach, such as teaching a unit in beanbags, which is content bound and quite limited.

The following structures, appropriate for use in physical education and used throughout the book, are based on work by Kagan (1992), Johnson and Johnson (1975), Johnson et al. (1984), Slavin (1980), Aronson (1978), and Orlick (1978, 1982).

Think-Share-Perform Based on Think-Pair-Share (Kagan 1992)

This is a strategy for encouraging participation through thinking, sharing, negotiating, and performing. It is particularly useful in creative dance, games, and obstacle courses, as well as in practicing game and sport strategies through problem solving lessons.

After co-developing a plan, students put the equipment in just the right place.

HOW TO:

1. Teacher provides a challenge.
2. Students individually think of possible answers.
3. Students share their responses with a partner.
4. Students perform at least one response from each partner and decide which response to perform in the activity.

For an example of Think-Share-Perform, see "Body Parts A' Movin'" on page 60.

Collective Score (Orlick 1982)

A method of cooperating in which all scores from all teams are added together for a collective total group score. Scores may be totaled in three ways:

1. Scores may be added for each group within a class.
2. All group scores may be added for a class score.
3. All class scores may be added for a total school score.

Collective score, for counting seconds or repetitions, can be used across a variety of activities, including team sports (e.g., volleyball), individual sports (e.g., racquetball), playground games (e.g., four square), gymnastics (e.g., cartwheels), physical fitness (e.g., push-ups) and motor skills (e.g., ball bouncing).

Students, in unison, move to scoop up as many balls as possible.

HOW TO:

1. Students perform specified skill or activity.
2. Each student counts his or her own repetitions.
3. Each student contributes his or her score toward the group total.
4. If goal setting is used, remember individuals cannot always perform more repetitions. Do not invite failure by telling groups that now the goal is higher than last time. Try setting a goal like, "Can your group do at least five less than your last total to as many as you can?" Or better yet, teach the students about goal setting (being reasonable) and allow them to set their own group goal.

The game "Bump Over" on page 86 uses Collective Score.

Jigsaw Perform Based on Jigsaw (Aronson 1978)

In this division of labor and sharing structure, each student is responsible for learning and performing a portion of the content and then teaching his or her portion to other group members. During Jigsaw Perform there is very strong positive interdependence as each student is totally dependent upon others for the information. One way to use Jigsaw Perform in physical education is for group teaching in games.

HOW TO:

1. Teacher assigns a task with several parts.
2. Each group member is responsible for learning and practicing one assigned part.

3. Each group member teaches or performs his or her assigned part to the group.

The Jigsaw Perform structure is used in the activity "Body Parts Aerobics" found on page 102.

Pairs-Check-Perform Based on Pairs Check (Kagan 1992)

Pairs-Check-Perform is a cooperative learning structure that requires individuals to stay on task and help others learn.

This structure is useful when learning any locomotor and manipulative skill, sport (e.g., track and field, paddle ball) and dance skill, gymnastic stunt, or aquatic skill.

HOW TO:
1. Teacher explains, demonstrates, and checks for understanding of the selected skill.
2. Teacher places students in groups of four, divided into two pairs.
3. In each pair, Student One practices the skill, while Student Two provides encouragement and help to correctly perform the skill.
4. When Student One has performed correctly, Student One becomes the encourager/helper, and Student Two becomes the performer.
5. When students in each pair have performed correctly, they join together with the other pair and each student from each pair performs. If all students agree that the performances were correct, the group may begin practicing the next skill; if there is disagreement, the students must continue working on the performance until all agree.

The game "Sportball Juggle" on page 76 uses the Pairs-Check-Perform structure.

Learning Teams Based on STAD (Slavin 1980) and Learning Together (Johnson and Johnson 1975)

Learning Teams provide students with opportunities to share leadership and responsibility and use collaborative skills to achieve group goals. Learning Teams are useful for skill acquisition in any content area of physical education.

HOW TO:
1. Teacher provides explanation, demonstration, and checking for understanding of selected skill.
2. Teacher tells students the performance outcome and social skills necessary for accomplishing this outcome.

3. Students are placed in groups of four.
4. Teachers assign specific roles for the activity:
   a. Performer
   b. Observer/checker
   c. Feedback provider
   d. Equipment retriever
5. Students carry out assigned roles during skill practice.
6. Students can be assessed by group members on skill performance.
7. Students are scored on an individual, group, or combination basis.

"21 Wall Ball" on page 80 can use the Learning Teams structure.

Co-op Play Based on Learning Together (Johnson et al. 1984 and Orlick 1978, 1982)

Co-op Play stresses working together to achieve a group goal through inclusive activities in which all students are involved and accepted. Co-op Play is an appropriate structure for modifying or creating games, dances, obstacle courses, and other skill development activities.

Under the guidance of the teacher, these students collectively decide how to make a challenging obstacle with their bodies.

HOW TO:

1. Teacher provides explanation and demonstration and checks for understanding of the activity or teaches through problem solving questions.
2. Teacher directly teaches necessary collaborative skills and emphasizes that without these skills the group will not be successful.
3. Teacher reinforces the idea that individual students can only be successful when all players are successful.
4. Students participate in the activity while teacher reinforces all skills and behaviors that will result in the group achieving their goal.
5. Following participation in the activity, teacher processes with the group why they were or were not successful.
6. Teacher encourages students to think about and share how goal achievement could be attained more easily or quickly.

The Co-op Play structure is used in the activity "Human Obstacle Course" on page 58.

Co-op Co-op Perform Based on Co-op Co-op (Kagan 1992)

Co-op Co-op Perform is a cooperative learning structure in which small groups are used to create a project that is shared with the rest of the class. This structure is useful in the areas of creative games and dance.

HOW TO:

1. A class discussion about the topic to be examined begins the lesson, for example, a theme for a dance.
2. The theme is divided into parts.
3. The teacher assigns each group a part of the theme.
4. Each group discusses the components of the part and decides how to perform these components.
5. Each group performs their part for the other groups.
6. Each part is linked with another part as practicing continues.
7. All parts are combined for a group performance.

An example activity using Co-op Co-op Perform is "Thunderstorm Dance" on page 92.

Through understanding and using structures such as those explained in this chapter, physical education teachers will be able to create new cooperative activities and modify existing activities to ensure maximal learning across the psychomotor, cognitive, and affective domains. Using these structures moves the teacher away from the limited activity-centered approach to an approach that can be applied across the entire physical education curriculum for all students.

Summary

It is of utmost importance that physical education be improved by renewing an emphasis on students and their learning. Cooperative learning is a way of thinking about and implementing physical education that can lead to improvements in teaching and learning. Forming teams, establishing positive interdependence, ensuring individual accountability, and developing collaborative skills are all necessary for cooperative learning.

Positive interdependence is the most important ingredient because it means that students need each other for learning and accomplishing instructional goals. Cooperative structures—or ways of organizing students for cooperative interaction during small group instruction—can be used to develop cooperative lessons. Several structures developed for use in the general education classroom have been modified for use in physical education. Teachers should use cooperative structures to develop varied lessons across the curriculum rather than using an activity-centered approach.

A Time to Reflect

1. Why do you want to become a physical education teacher? Are you interested in coaching? What conflicts do you perceive in attempting to be an effective teacher and coach? What do physical education and athletics share? What is different?

2. Look for examples of positive interdependence in the news media. If you found many examples, or did not, what does that mean? Do you think it is difficult for our culture to understand the idea of "sink or swim together"? Why or why not?

3. It is a well established fact that physical education can develop character and many other positive social skills. Does this really occur? Why or why not? Think about the activities you participated in during physical education and observe several physical education classes. Did the activities require positive social skills? What did the teacher do to encourage or discourage these skills?

4. Go to the library and complete a data-based search to learn more about cooperative learning and cooperative structures. Read five different articles and describe how this information can be applied to teaching and learning in physical education. Ask other teachers to share cooperative learning structures/activities that work with their students. Which do you think you could try? Take a risk and try!

References

Aronson, E. 1978. *The jigsaw classroom*. Beverly Hills, CA: Sage.

Chu, D. 1980. A sociological analysis of the career lives of American physical education teachers and coaches. *Abstracts: International Congress on Women in Sport*. Rome, Italy, 4-5.

Colby, M., B. Steir, and J. Jensen. 1994. *Conference proceedings on the future of physical education*. Brockport, New York: Department of Physical Education and Sport.

Grineski, S. 1994. The image and future of physical education: Cultural inertia. In *Conference proceedings on the future of physical education*, edited by M. Colby, B. Steir, and J. Jensen, 13-14. Brockport, New York: Department of Physical Education and Sport.

Johnson, D., and R. Johnson. 1975. *Learning together and alone*. Englewood Cliffs, NJ: Prentice-Hall.

Johnson, D., R. Johnson, E. Holubec, and P. Roy. 1984. *Circles of learning*. Alexandria, VA: Association for Supervision and Development.

Kagan, S. 1992. *Cooperative learning*. San Juan Capistrano, CA: Kagan Cooperative Learning.

Kneer, M. 1994. The future of physical education. In *Conference proceedings on the future of physical education*, edited by M. Colby, B. Steir, and J. Jensen, 3-4. Brockport, New York: Department of Physical Education and Sport.

National Association for Sport and Physical Education (NASPE). 1992. *Developmentally appropriate physical education practices for children: A position statement of the National Association for Sport and Physical Education/ Developed by the Council on Physical Education for Children*. Reston, VA: AAHPERD.

———. 1992. *The physically educated person*. Reston, VA: AAHPERD.

———. 1995. *Moving into the future: National standards for physical education. A guide to content and assessment*. St. Louis: Mosby.

Orlick, T. 1978. *The cooperative sports and games book*. New York: Pantheon.

———. 1982. *The second cooperative sports and games book*. New York: Pantheon.

Seagrave, T. 1987. Cited by M. Kneer. 1994. In *Conference proceedings on the future of physical education*, edited by M. Colby, B. Steir, and J. Jensen, 3-4. Brockport, New York: Department of Physical Education and Sport.

Slavin, R. 1980. *Using student team learning*. Baltimore: The Center for Social Organization of Schools, The Johns Hopkins University.

Wang, M., G. Haaertel, and H. Walberg. 1994. What helps students learn? *Educational Leadership* (January): 74-79.

CHAPTER 3

Making Instructional Decisions for Cooperative Learning

Now the process of using cooperative learning begins. As described in chapter 1, quality physical education is goal-directed, increasing the likelihood that children will become skillful, physically fit, knowledgeable, and caring movers. Quality physical education can be put into practice through cooperative learning so that these outcomes will occur. Of course, "into practice" means making instructional decisions about planning, teaching, and evaluating.

Planning Cooperative Learning Lessons

If you are new to cooperative physical education, begin by using activities from chapters 4-8 that fit in with your existing curriculum plans. For example, if you are planning activities for children in first grade around the theme of body and spatial awareness, include some activities from chapter 4—Cooperative Learning: Movement Concept and Motor Skill Development. You might choose "Body Parts A' Movin'," a developmentally appropriate cooperative activity that uses the Co-op Play structure. It is designed to develop the following goal areas: enhance body and spatial awareness, encourage creativity, and promote cooperation with peers. Thus, "Body Parts A' Movin'" develops the student's psychomotor, cognitive, and affective abilities.

In small groups, students move through the space, starting and stopping with music, while following challenges provided by the teacher. "Can your group move with

1. three feet on the ground?
2. hands on ankles?
3. five body parts on the ground?"

Experiencing cooperative learning in this way will allow you and your students to start slowly, yet be successful. Remember to think about and to discuss with the students the effects of cooperative learning in physical education. When your skill and confidence increase, you will find that the activities in this text are an excellent resource and that the structures discussed earlier can guide you in designing your personal approach to cooperative physical education learning.

Modifying Existing Lessons to Be Cooperative

As you begin to practice cooperative learning, you will want to examine existing lessons and determine if a cooperative learning structure would result in quality physical education. The following is a framework, with examples, for modifying existing lessons by placing them into cooperative learning structures.

1. Choose instructional goals in the psychomotor, cognitive, and affective domains and select an activity designed to achieve these goals that feels especially comfortable to you.

Example:

Goals

Psychomotor: To improve endurance
              To improve arm and shoulder strength

Cognitive: To promote problem solving

Affective: To enhance positive social interaction

Content Area: Physical Fitness Activity Obstacle Course

2. Observe and analyze the way students are currently organized for interaction during learning. Watch them work and ask yourself, "Is each child practicing alone? Are they working in groups? Are learning opportunities contingent on skill, gender, or luck? Are children competing against one another or a group?" One method of observation is to scan from left to right while students are involved in the activity and count how many chil-

dren are actually performing the target skills. Another is to randomly ask children to perform the skill.

Example: Students are individually participating in an obstacle course. Obstacles include running in and out, jumping over, pushing a heavy object, swinging from a rope, riding a scooter board, and jumping, hopping, and leaping on floor marks. Each student works very hard when it is his or her turn, but receives only one turn every eight minutes. You do not observe any interaction while students are performing in the obstacle course.

3. If the existing goal structure results in only a few students achieving a minimal number of instructional goals with limited enjoyment, select a cooperative structure that would increase the number of students learning and enjoying. If appropriate, use simple structures initially. For example, with physical fitness or skill practice activities, try Collective Score, and for games, try Co-op Play.

Example: In using the structure Co-op Play for the obstacle course, students are placed in heterogeneous groups of four, with hands joined, and instructed to negotiate the course as quickly as possible. The group goal is to move through the course without knocking over any obstacles while keeping all hands joined. You may also time the group.

4. Use this activity again with the new structure and determine if more students are learning and enjoying the activity. Use similar methods for observing.

5. If successful, great; if not, try another structure.

Example: The structure Co-op Play resulted in more opportunities for each student to go through the course and, as a result, more opportunities to achieve the intended goals.

Creating Cooperative Lessons

After becoming comfortable using cooperative activities and competent in modifying existing activities through cooperative structures, you are ready for the next step. This step is selecting the appropriate structure(s) for specific instructional goals and matching activities across your curriculum. Here is how to accomplish this step:

1. Identify the instructional goals from the psychomotor, cognitive, and affective domains that you want the activity to accomplish.
2. Select the appropriate structure(s).

Use the following diagram to maximize learning:

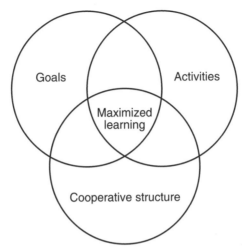

Goals + Activities + Cooperative structures = Maximized learning

This formula can be used to develop unlimited cooperative physical education activities that are not bound by content. Within the cooperative learning field, at least 100 different structures (Kagan 1992) are available, and many can be adapted for use in organizing cooperative learning in physical education. As you continue to use cooperative learning in your program, you will become more confident and competent and begin to modify and create structures to better meet the needs of more students.

Teaching for Cooperation: Teaching Practices

Once the instructional goal(s), appropriate structure(s), and activities are selected, teachers need to decide how best to teach the structure and content. Although a discussion of managing the lesson is beyond the scope of this book, you can find an excellent treatment of the subject in Graham (1992).

Four Basic Ideas

Four important ideas about cooperation guide teachers during a cooperative learning lesson:

1. Students need to understand that cooperation means everybody achieves the goal when all students contribute to goal achievement.
2. The goal and methods for accomplishing the goal have to be meaningful and motivating to the students.
3. The teacher needs to emphasize and facilitate affective skills so students understand how important they are for group goal achievement.
4. The teacher needs to teach, use, and reinforce cooperative vocabulary.

During activities with cooperative goal structures, each student's contribution is necessary for goal achievement.

Beginning and Ending

These four important ideas can be applied to two vital lesson components: *set to learn* and *closure*.

Set to Learn

The set to learn is the initial lesson activity used to describe the day's learning, provide a purpose, and get the students excited about learning. This activity sets the stage for learning and motivates students. Some set to learn ideas used for describing cooperation are

- children playing on a teeter-totter,
- firefighters working together in putting out a fire,
- musicians playing a piece of music together, and
- actors, director, and producer making a movie.

Closure

Use the following ideas to close a lesson and reinforce the importance of working together:

- Ask children if everybody received many turns and if not what could have been done differently.
- Identify actions that helped players work hard and feel good.
- Use phrases that reinforce desired behaviors (e.g., "Let's use encouraging words, not discouraging words.").

INSIGHTS FROM THE GYM

Six fifth-graders were playing the "Keep It Up" game, which requires six players to hold hands in a circle and keep a beach ball up in the air by lightly tapping the ball with joined arms and hands. As students were tapping the ball in the air, Jon said, "That's it! We are doing great." The group shouted, "We're doing it!" The ball suddenly fell to the ground when Bill did not hit the ball with the person next to him. Seeing Bill's failure to keep the ball up, Sue exclaimed, "You dummy! You made the ball fall!" When the teacher heard these words, she asked Sue what the goal of the activity was and what were ways to accomplish this goal. The teacher then reminded Sue of the importance of using encouraging rather than discouraging words. Sue thought for a moment and said, "O.K., everybody, let's work together and keep that ball up in the air."

During cooperative lessons, teachers should circulate, providing feedback on the important motor, cognitive, and affective skills required for goal achievement. Teachers also play a crucial role in modeling appropriate behavior. The children must know that the teacher values cooperative learning and the effort, whatever it may be, given by each student.

Teaching for Cooperation: Teaching Styles

When presenting cooperative activities to students, teachers need to clearly teach information regarding cooperative structure(s) and content.

Problem Solving

The problem solving style of teaching, that is, encouraging divergent thinking through use of open-ended questions, is one teaching style that can be used (Mosston and Ashworth 1994). This student-centered way of teaching encourages creativity and problem solving.

When to Use Problem Solving

During a cooperative lesson, problem solving is appropriate when the teacher wants students to

- create a dance, game, or obstacle course;
- explore movement concepts like general space, pathways, and levels;
- explore motor skills like throwing, catching, and kicking; or
- devise new strategies for group games or sports.

INSIGHTS FROM THE GYM

A teacher trying to encourage problem solving with third-grade children asked the following problem solving questions.

"Can you and your partner move fast through the space while making at least three direction and three level changes?"

"Try using your four bodies to make playground equipment. You can work with other groups if you want. Think about the shape of the equipment and how much space the equipment takes up."

"How many different bridges can you and your partner make in 60 seconds? Be prepared to tell me about or show me at least five. Try to build bridges using some of our movement concepts words—level, pathways, direction."

Working collectively, students can create wonderful solutions to movement tasks.

Framework for Problem Solving

In order to use problem solving, teachers need to ask open-ended questions that are stimulating and exciting for students. Teachers must plan these questions in advance, as it is difficult to think of effective problem solving questions on the spot in front of thirty students. Follow these steps to come up with good questions:

1. Select an instructional goal.

   Example: Locomotor skills

2. Identify a skill within the goal area.

   Example: Jumping

3. With this skill in mind, write questions that result in unlimited answers. Follow steps a through d.

   a. Begin question with an introductory phrase that invites divergent thinking.

      Example: How would you and your partner? What if you and your partner? How many can you and your partner? Can you and your partner?

   b. After the introductory phrase, add the skill.

      Example: How would you jump?

   c. Following the introductory phrase and skill, use movement concepts that will allow for a variety of answers.

      Example: How would you jump in different directions, really hard and as fast as you can?

   d. Enrich the question with a meaningful and age appropriate child-centered context or theme.

      Example: Pretend you are rabbit friends being chased in a forest full of trees by a very large bear. How would you two jump so you didn't bump into any trees and didn't get bitten by the bear?

Jumping can even be done in groups of four!

The Direct Style

Another style of teaching that is useful in teaching cooperative structures and content is the direct style of teaching. The direct style elicits convergent thinking through the use of verbal statements, demonstrations, and checking for understanding with statements and questions (Mosston and Ashworth 1994). This is a teacher-directed style based on the idea of stimulus by the teacher and response by the student.

When to Use the Direct Style

Teaching cooperative structures, motor skills, social skills, and strategies to students for the first time can be done effectively through the direct style of teaching. In addition, any activity or structure with many and/or sophisticated components can be taught with the direct style. Effective use of the direct style of teaching depends on clear verbal cues, specific modeling, and accurate checking for understanding.

Framework for Direct Style

To practice the direct style of teaching, follow these steps:

1. Select an instructional goal.

   Example: Sport skills

2. Identify a skill within the goal area.

   Example: Layup shot

3. Task analyze the skill into three to five components.

   Example: 1. Step 2. Hop 3. Push

4. For each component write out a verbal statement you can use with your students (i.e., TELL), a description of the visual demonstration you are planning (i.e., SHOW), and how you will check for understanding (i.e., CHECK).

   Example: Component Part: TELL SHOW CHECK (see p. 48)

   Have each student say three parts to self and practice layups, concentrating on step-hop-push. Teacher gives feedback on these parts.

Component	Tell	Show	Check
Step	Step forward straight.	Straight step.	All perform with left foot step straight if shooting with right hand.
Hop	Stand on foot and bounce into the air with soft landing. Left foot if shooting with left hand.	Bounce into air with soft landing.	All perform hop on correct foot.
Push	With ball in shooting hand, shoot ball to basket by straightening elbow, pushing ball toward basket, and snapping wrist down.	Straighten, push, snap.	Ask students for three key words.

The Role of the Teacher

Teachers play an important role during the cooperative lesson. Based on instructional decisions made prior to the lesson, they should make every effort to explain with clarity, model carefully, check to make sure students understand, ask thought-provoking questions, and reinforce all positive behaviors. Effective teaching is always difficult, but when it results in student learning, it is a job with many rewards.

Evaluating Cooperative Learning

After planning and teaching cooperative physical education lessons, teachers need to think reflectively in order to answer the following evaluation questions:

- Did the students learn?
- How much did the students learn?
- Were the students helpful in assisting others to learn?
- Did the students enjoy learning?

Based on the answers to these questions the teacher can decide to eliminate a lesson, keep a lesson intact, or change part or parts of the lesson by evaluating instructional goals, goal structure, activities, teaching behaviors, and teaching style. Two steps for evaluating a lesson include assessment and analysis.

Assessment

Teachers can assess the motor, cognitive, and affective performance of children in several ways:

- Use the left to right scan while the children are involved in the activity and count how many children are performing the specified skills correctly.
- Randomly select a group of children and count how many times they perform a specified skill.
- Randomly select a few children and ask them to explain how to perform the skill or some aspect of cooperating in the group.
- Have the children teach a peer or younger child the specified skill.
- Have the children describe in writing the specified skill or some aspect of cooperating.
- Briefly participate with the children to get a feel for their performances.
- Design a series of stations centered on the specified skills with the teacher observing and using a checklist to record performance data at one station. The children rotate through all stations.

It is also important for the teacher to assess use of teaching styles and interactions with children. This can be done through analysis:

- Self-analysis following lessons,
- Asking students, peers, or the principal for feedback, and
- Using videotape to systematically analyze the lesson.

Analysis

After you have collected information through assessment, you can decide how to improve teaching and learning. If the assessment information indicates that many students appear to be learning, keep up the good work; if not, begin thinking about what modifications need to occur. The following questions may be useful in modifying lessons:

- Are the instructional goals age appropriate for the group?
- Were the instructional goals the most important goals to be learned by this group of children?
- Was the number of instructional goals appropriate?
- Did the activity allow for maximum learning opportunities with a high degree of success for many students? Was it open-ended to allow for individual differences?
- Did the sequence of activities preceding this lesson provide the skill practice necessary to be successful in the lesson?
- Was the cooperative structure appropriate for the students and activity?
- Was the instruction for the cooperative structure and activity clear and understood by the students?
- While the students were participating in the lesson, did the teacher circulate throughout the gym and teach, model, and reinforce appropriate collaborative skills?

When cooperative learning activities are taught effectively, students of all ages can learn and have fun.

Evaluating is essential for teachers who want to improve teaching so more students learn. This is particularly true for physical education teachers who are beginning to use cooperative learning. Try selecting one method of evaluation and use it regularly for a period of time. Think about the results generated from these observations. Make changes slowly and thoughtfully and enjoy the confidence you gain as your competence increases. For more information concerning planning, teaching, and evaluating see Graham (1992).

Summary

Instructional decision making is a process of planning, teaching, and evaluating intended to affect student learning positively. These instructional components can be adapted specifically to cooperative learning in physical education. Either the problem solving style or the direct style of teaching is appropriate for achieving quality physical education. But no matter what style is chosen, the teacher's role in modeling and reinforcing appropriate behavior and proper skill practice is critical to success. Assessment and analysis is also vital to quality physical education and can be achieved by using techniques and questions listed in the chapter.

A Time to Reflect

Think about your school experiences. How were you taught? Think about teachers across various subject areas and ages and observe how they are teaching. How many teachers used questions to teach? If many did, why do you think they did? If many did not, why do you think they did not? Which way of teaching do you enjoy? How will you teach?

References

Graham, G. 1992. *Teaching children physical education—Becoming a master teacher.* Champaign, IL: Human Kinetics.

Kagan, S. 1992. *Cooperative learning.* San Juan Capistrano, CA: Kagan Cooperative Learning.

Mosston, M., and S. Ashworth. 1994. *Teaching physical education.* 3d ed. Columbus, OH: Merrill.

CHAPTER 4

Cooperative Learning: Movement Concept and Motor Skill Development

As the students entered the gymnasium, some feelings of anxiety filled the air. They knew they were going to learn and practice the overhand throwing skill today, and if ready, use the skill in the activity. The instructor requested each student to stand near a bucket of yarn balls, arm's-length apart, and face the front wall. Using the direct style of teaching, the teacher explained, demonstrated, and checked understanding of the component parts of the skill: elbow back, step forward, and throw hard.

Following instruction, the students began to overhand throw yarn balls at wall targets. Students, working in pairs, started at a distance of 20 feet from the wall, and moved back five feet when they could successfully hit the wall target three out of five times. The teacher encouraged the students to help their partners throw better by providing feedback on the component parts.

As the students practiced, the teacher circulated and provided visual and verbal cues regarding their performances. He was surprised at what he observed. Many of the students did not understand how their body parts worked with other parts, as well as how they worked in isolation from other parts. Some students exhibited an awkward throwing pattern, demonstrating little fluidity in their motion. In addition, a number of students had difficulty in judging distance and applying appropriate force when throwing. The teacher concluded that this group of students was not ready to participate in an organized activity using the overhand throwing skill.

The teacher had made similar observations in the past with young children, but never with adults. This, however, was not a primary grade physical education class, but a teacher preparation class in Elementary Physical Education for Elementary Education majors. He wondered, "Is this what happens if children are not allowed to acquire movement concepts and motor skills?" Do they grow into adults who exhibit delayed motor development that inhibits basic motor skill acquisition? Upon questioning the students, the teacher found that the majority had not received instruction in movement concepts nor basic motor skills as children. As a result, many of them avoided movement related activities as adults.

This is a true story that has been repeated many times in the classes I teach.

Important Learning for Children: Movement Concepts

Movement concepts include body awareness, spatial awareness, and effort awareness. These concepts are the building blocks for learning in physical education, and they govern performance of motor skills in all physical activity. Efficient and effective use of movement concepts allows students to use motor skills in a variety of ways and across many different conditions and environments.

Body Awareness

Concepts of body awareness include identifying body parts and having a familiarity with different body shapes. Content associated with body shapes includes being able to assume shapes such as round, curled, twisted, narrow, and wide. Understanding the movements of body parts and the relationships of body parts while moving are additional body awareness concepts.

Spatial Awareness

Spatial awareness is understanding the relationship between the body and space. The major spatial awareness concepts are

1. self-space, or personal space;
2. general space, or space for movement;
3. level, or space in terms of height—high, medium, low;

4. direction, or space regarding body movement—forward, backward, right, left, up, and down; and
5. pathways, or space for lines of movement—straight, curvy, zigzag, and combinations.

Effort Awareness

Effort awareness may be thought of in terms of the qualitative aspects of movement: time, force, and flow. Movement may be fast and sudden or slow and controlled, heavy and strong, or light and easy. Movement may also be performed in a restricted and tight fashion or in an easy and smooth style.

These three movement concepts provide the foundation for skill acquisition in physical education. Understanding how the body works as it moves through space allows the student to perform a variety of skills with greater efficiency and effectiveness.

Important Learning for Children: Motor Skills

Development of motor skills is one of the primary goals of physical education. These skills, in combination with movement concepts, provide the basis for meaningful and successful participation in physical activity.

Locomotor Skills

Locomotor skills are those goal-directed movement patterns used to move the body through space. Each skill has been analyzed into task relevant cues for teaching since cues assist learners in performing locomotor skills. Walking and running have simple descriptions instead of cues. Locomotor skills include the following:

- Walking—moving with one foot in front of the other, while keeping one foot in contact with the ground at all times
- Running—moving with one foot in front of the other, with short periods of time when neither foot is on the ground
- Hopping— same foot/ bounce, bounce, bounce . . .
- Jumping—both feet/up and down
- Galloping—one foot lead/one foot follow
- Sliding—step/together
- Leaping—take off one foot/land with other foot, then the first
- Skipping—step/hop and step/hop

Manipulative Skills

Manipulative skills are those goal-directed movement patterns used to propel and receive objects. Each skill has been analyzed into task relevant cues for teaching as use of cues assists learners in performing manipulative skills. Manipulative skills include the following:

- Overhand throw—step/elbow back/throw hard/step
- Catch—look/grab/hug
- Hand strike—look/step/swing-strike/step
- Hand dribble—look/bent knees/tap
- Kick—look/step/swing-kick/follow through
- Punt—look/step/drop/swing-punt/follow through

Participating in planned physical education experiences that are skill-directed and rich in movement concepts enables students to experience quality learning in physical education.

Cooperative Learning Activities
for the Movement Concept and Motor Skill Development Program

Locomotor Moving
I

Activity Challenge: To respond appropriately to directives from Locomotor Moving Cards

Description: Pairs of students receive a Locomotor Moving Card. Printed on each card is a number (e.g., 21), list of movement concepts (e.g., level, pathways, force), and locomotor skills (e.g., jump, run). Individual members think of how to use the specified movement concepts while performing the specified locomotor skills so they cumulatively add to the number on the card. Each member shares their idea and a decision is reached on how to respond to the Locomotor Moving Card. Students can combine ideas, reach consensus on an idea, or take turns using different ideas. Together they complete the task by putting all their ideas into action.

Equipment: Five different Locomotor Moving Cards per group

Psychomotor Goal: Improve locomotor skills

Cognitive Goal: Enhance decision making

Affective Goal: Use positive interactions to collectively plan and move

Variations: When students can successfully respond to Locomotor Moving Cards in pairs, increase group size. Ask students to move to various pieces of music. Students can create their own Locomotor Moving Cards and share with classmates. Students can perform their movements and have classmates guess what number and which movement concepts and motor skills are on their card.

Cooperative Learning Structure: Think-Share-Perform

Human Obstacle Course

Activity Challenge: To maintain and negotiate obstacles for a predetermined amount of time

Description: Students in small groups make obstacles using their joined bodies. The obstacles should be spread throughout the play space. The remaining players, in groups and holding hands, attempt to negotiate the obstacles without touching any obstacle.

Equipment: None

Psychomotor Goals: Enhance body and spatial awareness

Cognitive Goal: Encourage problem solving

Affective Goal: Use positive interactions to maintain obstacles and move without touching obstacles

Variations: Begin with groups of two players and expand to larger groups of up to five players when students can successfully maintain and negotiate larger obstacles. Use a variety of movement concepts in building obstacles. For example, wide-narrow, tall-short, high-medium-low, and curvy-straight. Different body parts could also be used to form obstacles (i.e., hands, feet, elbows). Teachers can instruct students who are negotiating obstacles to move in forward, sideways, or backward directions and at different speeds.

Cooperative Learning Structure: Co-op Play (Collective Score could also be used with the number of obstacles negotiated in a certain time counted.)

Body Parts A' Movin'

Activity Challenge: To move in groups a specified distance while responding correctly to challenges given by the teacher

Description: Students in groups of three move throughout the play space starting and stopping with music. While moving together, the group attempts to follow challenges provided by the teacher:

Move with

- three feet touching the ground with hands on ankles,
- five body parts on the ground,
- some body parts at a medium level and some parts at a low level,
- all players on their side and connected to each other,
- one person at a low level and two persons at a high level,
- all players making a round and low shape,
- lots of noise without using feet or mouths,
- all backs touching and very fast, and
- body parts being used so the group looks like a spider.

Equipment: Record: Hap Palmer, "Movin'," AR546, Educational Activities, Freeport, NY 11520

Psychomotor Goals: Enhance body and spatial awareness

Cognitive Goal: Encourage creativity

Affective Goal: Use positive interactions to accomplish challenges

Variations: After players successfully accomplish a specified number of challenges, try increasing the number of players in each group. Introduce various pieces of equipment for use in accomplishing a challenge. For example, players, without use of hands, hold a rope and move in a curvy pathway. Vary the distance and pathway groups must travel to be successful. Ask students to create new challenges.

Cooperative Learning Structure: Think-Share-Perform

Under the Rope

I

Activity Challenge: To have all players pass under a suspended rope and hold a suspended rope without the use of hands

Description: Two students hold a 10-foot jump rope while remaining group members move or cross under the rope. None of the students are allowed to touch the rope with their hands. Students rotate positions so all receive a turn holding and moving under the rope.

Equipment: One 10-foot rope per group of students

Psychomotor Goals: Enhance body and spatial awareness

Cognitive Goal: Promote decision making

Affective Goal: Use positive interactions to successfully have group hold rope and move under rope

Variations: Try limiting use of other body parts (e.g., feet) or combinations of body parts (e.g., right hand, left elbow, and both feet). Have students use a shorter rope or work in smaller or larger groups. Systematically rotate students through various groups; this requires using other cooperative learning structures, such as Think-Share-Perform and Jigsaw Perform. The teacher may limit the amount of time allotted to achieving the goal. This strategy could be used in conjunction with the Collective Score structure with group scores added together.

Cooperative Learning Structure: Co-op Play (Other structures could be used as noted in "Variations.")

Wand Grabbing

Activity Challenge: To trade places with your partner without either wand falling on the ground

Description: Students in pairs stand five feet apart and vertically hold a 3-foot wand on the floor. On an agreed signal, all students let go of their wands and run to grab the wands of their partners. Teachers should remind students to keep their heads up and eyes fixed on their partners' wands when changing places with their partners.

Equipment: One 3-foot wand for each student

Psychomotor Goal: Enhance effort awareness

Cognitive Goals: Promote negotiating behaviors
Stimulate problem solving skills

Affective Goal: Use positive interactions to grab partner's wand before it touches the ground

Variations: After pairs of students develop skill in releasing and grabbing, increase the distance between the students. Also, students may work in groups larger than pairs. It is challenging to work toward an entire class of students releasing and grabbing simultaneously. Once students experience success with the activity, introduce the cooperative learning structure Collective Score. To use Collective Score in the Wand Grabbing activity, students increase the distance from their partner by one foot when they can successfully grab their partner's wand three times in a row. The "score" would be how far apart partners are at the end of a specified time. This distance could be added for a class total.

Cooperative Learning Structure: Think-Share-Perform (Collective Score can also be used as noted in "Variations.")

Cut the Pizza

Activity Challenge: To have entire class run through the center of a circle (i.e., cut the pizza) without touching other students

Description: Students in a large group run around the outside of a circle (i.e., the pizza) approximately 40 feet in diameter. On command of "Cut the Pizza," students run through the center of the circle and then through a smaller concentric circle approximately 10 feet in diameter. Students attempt to cut or cross through the center of the small circle and return to running around the large circle without touching any classmates.

Equipment: Two circles marked on the floor, a large circle approximately 40 feet in diameter, and a smaller concentric circle approximately 10 feet in diameter

Psychomotor Goals: Enhance body and spatial awareness
Enhance effort awareness
Improve locomotor skills

Cognitive Goal: Promote problem solving skills

Affective Goal: To use positive interactions to encourage and facilitate fellow students to cross through circle without touching others

Variations: Increase or decrease the size of the circles. Change locomotor skill used when crossing the circles. Consider matching a specific locomotor skill to each of the two circles. For example, students gallop around the large circle and then change to skipping when crossing through the small circle. Have students move through the circles in groups of two, three, or four. Try requiring the students to be moving backward or sideways when running around the large circle or when crossing through the small circle.

Cooperative Learning Structure: Co-op Play

Hoopin' Together

Activity Challenge: To move a hoop around a circle of players who are holding hands

Description: Students holding hands in groups of six attempt to pass a hula hoop from one player to the next without letting go of hands. The hula hoop must pass over the players' bodies. Once students can successfully pass a hoop around the circle three times without error, provide the following challenges:

Pass the hoop around the circle

- with eyes closed;
- without talking;
- facing away from center;
- standing on one foot;
- jumping through the hoop;
- two, three, four, or five students at the same time;
- hoop remaining still with students moving;
- specific body part leading through the hoop;
- from a kneeling, sitting, or lying position; and
- as fast or as slow as possible.

Equipment: Several hoops of different sizes for each circle of students

Psychomotor Goals: Enhance body and spatial awareness

Cognitive Goals: Encourage creativity and problem solving

Affective Goal: Use positive interactions to move hoop around the circle

Variations: After trying the 10 challenges provided, think of new ones, or try the challenges using smaller groups, adding hoops, or working for speed.

Cooperative Learning Structure: Co-op Play (Collective Score could be used if hoop passing is timed.)

(Pangrazi and Dauer 1995)

21 Frantic Ball

Activity Challenge: To stay as close as possible to the score of 21 points

Description: Students run while holding hands with a partner and attempt to keep all balls moving that have been previously scattered throughout the play space. Students may only contact balls with their hands. When the teacher observes a ball not moving, she calls "ball" and a point is deducted from the beginning class group total of 21 points. All students attempt to stay as close as possible to the class total of 21 points. The teacher can use a left to right scan of the play space or interval observing for scoring points. This latter technique is accomplished by observing and counting in one-fourth of the gymnasium for 10 seconds then switching and observing another section of the gymnasium for 10 seconds and so on. Student cooperation is more important than exact scoring, although students are interested in scoring activities.

The following sequence is suggested for learning to play "21 Frantic Ball":

1. Small groups of students straddle-sitting on floor attempt to keep 4 to 10 balls moving.
2. Small groups of students standing in place attempt to keep 4 to 10 balls moving. Students are allowed to take one pivot step to reach and strike balls.
3. Small groups of students playing in one-fourth of the play space attempt to run and keep 8 to 20 balls moving.
4. Pairs of students who are holding hands attempt to keep 5 to 10 balls moving in one-fourth of the play space.

Equipment: 40 balls of different sizes

Psychomotor Goals: Improve spatial awareness
Improve manipulative skills

Cognitive Goal: Enhance problem solving skills

Affective Goal: Use positive interactions to move with partner and tap balls

Variations: Increase or decrease size of play space. Use balls of varying weights. Change grouping size from two to six. Allow students to use different body parts to strike balls or to use striking implements, such as paddles.

Cooperative Learning Structure: Co-op Play (Think-Share-Perform may be used to determine better strategies to keep balls moving.)

(Torbert and Schneider 1994)

Partner Cards

Activity Challenge: To collectively perform the prescribed skill or activity with a partner

Description: 15 to 20 8- by 11-inch Partner Cards are scattered, with directions facing down, in the middle of the play space. Students in pairs select a Partner Card, turn the card over, and read the directions. The paired students find an area in the play space that is not crowded and attempt to satisfy the directions on the card. Safely distribute required equipment for each activity throughout the play space. All directions must be written in such a way that it is impossible for one student to satisfy the directions: Create positive interdependence. When placing appropriate equipment throughout the play space, provide pathways for moving-type activities and more secluded space for in-place activities.

The following is a list of possible activities:

1. Do one minute of partner straddle stretch.
2. Bounce and catch a ball 150 times.
3. Do 150 fast and slow Collective Score jumping jacks.
4. Partner hop 20 times. (Face partner and hold onto the leg of your partner. Hop together on supporting legs.)

5. Do a 150 Collective Score jump rope (one individual rope per two children).
6. Do two minutes of "Foot Tag." (Face partner and try to tag partner's foot with your foot.)

7. Do partner jumping in and out of hoops five times. (Hold hands with partner and jump at the same time.)
8. Do 10 games of "Leap Frog" across the play space.
9. Play "Wring the Dishrag" 10 times. (Face partner, hold hands, and turn back to back, then return to the original position.)

When students have successfully satisfied the directions of a Partner Card, they return the card face down in the center of play space and select a new card. Hint: To give your cards years of use, try laminating them.

Equipment: A set of Partner Cards and necessary equipment

Psychomotor Goal: Improve specific movement concepts and/or motor skills as noted on Partner Card

Cognitive Goal: Understand biomechanics (i.e., how the body moves while performing a skill) of motor skills performed

Affective Goal: Use positive interactions to teach partner and support partner's efforts

Variation: You can teach or reinforce any desired movement concept or motor skill through this activity for students of varying developmental levels. Incorporate any appropriate physical fitness activity to vary Partner Cards, for example, 150 Collective Score partner push-ups.

Cooperative Learning Structure: A variety of structures can be used for this activity. For learning concepts or skills, try Think-Share-Perform, Learning Teams, and Pairs-Check-Perform. Once students have learned the concept or skill, try Collective Score and/or Co-op Play.

How Long Can We?

P

Activity Challenge: To move collectively as far as possible with team-mates

Description: Students, in groups of three to six, stand in a straight line and individually horizontally jump as far as possible. Jumper One takes off from a starting line and jumps as far as possible. Each subsequent jumper begins his or her jump at the point where the preceding jumper landed. When all have jumped, the distance is recorded. Groups can repeat the process in trying to maintain or extend their jumping distance. Distances can be added together for a class score. Class scores could be added for a grade level score and grade level scores could be added for a total school score. This activity provides the teacher with the opportunity to make connections between learning in physical education and learning in other school subjects, such as mathematics or science.

Equipment: Measuring and marking devices

Psychomotor Goal: Improve locomotor skills

Cognitive Goal: Understand force production

Affective Goals: Use positive interactions in teaching teammates to jump further
Use positive interactions to support teammates' jumping efforts

Variations: This activity can also be used to practice and refine other locomotor skills, such as hopping and leaping.

Cooperative Learning Structure: Collective Score

(Orlick 1978)

Sneakin' Through the Front Door   P

Activity Challenge: To move under a swinging rope while holding hands in as large a group as possible

Description: Beginning with students paired and holding hands, students sneak (i.e., run) under a long jump rope that is being turned. After sufficient practice, change grouping pattern to four students holding hands and running under the rope. Continue practicing and increasing size of the groups. Students may need prompts to help them to know when to "sneak under." As students' skill levels increase, work toward using a longer rope and as many students as possible.

Equipment: Several long jump ropes

Psychomotor Goals: Improve spatial awareness
Improve effort awareness

Cognitive Goal: Increase understanding of timing

Affective Goal: Use positive interactions to move collectively and at the same speed

Variations: Changing locomotor skill (e.g., hopping) or means of locomotion, such as riding a scooter.

Cooperative Learning Structure: Co-op Play (Think-Share-Perform could be used in developing skills needed for successful participation. Collective Score could be used if scoring was used in determining how many individuals crossed under the rope at one time.)

References

Grineski, S. 1991a. *Dance education curriculum guide.* Bismarck, ND: Department of Public Instruction.

———. 1991b. Promoting success in physical education: Cooperatively structured learning. *PALAESTRA* 7(2): 26-29.

———. 1994. Cooperative fitness activities. *Teaching Elementary Physical Education* 5(1): 14-15.

Orlick, T. 1978. *The cooperative sports and games book.* New York: Pantheon.

Pangrazi, R., and V. Dauer. 1995. *Dynamic physical education for elementary school children.* 11th ed. Boston: Allyn and Bacon.

Torbert, M., and L. Schneider. 1994. *Follow me: A handbook for movement activities.* Philadelphia: The Leonard Gordon Institute for Human Development Through Play.

CHAPTER 5

Cooperative Learning: Games Education

"Do you remember the games we played in second grade?" asked Mary.

"I sure do," said Jose. "All we did was play Jump the Shot, Kickball, Softball, and Dodgeball."

"Yeah, and we sure stood around a lot. It got kinda boring," Mary replied. "I remember lots of arguing and fighting. John was really picked on. I don't think he ever got to play much."

"How about that Bombardment game?" Jose asked. "It seems like kids were always getting hurt and some kids didn't get how to play. I am glad we don't have to do that anymore."

"I really like playing games this year," Mary said. "We get to choose games a lot and even make up rules and stuff."

"What I really like are the games where we all get lots of turns and work together to win," Jose declared. "Even if some kids complain, I like not having to worry so much about winning. It makes it better."

"My favorite is 'Sportball Juggle,'" said Mary. "What's your favorite?"

"I like 'Towel Ball,'" said Jose.

"I wonder what the games will be like next year?" asked Mary.

Games Education

Games can make valuable contributions to the psychomotor, cognitive, and affective development of children. They can provide

- acquisition of motor skills and enhancement of physical fitness,
- development of positive social behaviors,
- enhancement of problem solving and creativity,
- promotion of verbal skills, and
- opportunities for fun and excitement.

What Makes a Game Educational?

A game is a rule-bound contest in which players attempt to achieve a goal. Although the value of games may not be inherent in the games themselves, games become educational when the following criteria are met:

- Educational purpose—the game will improve one or more areas of development
- Child-centered—the demands of the game match the child's level of development
- Problem solving—the game allows players to plan, analyze, create, and modify
- Positive socialization—the game promotes the development of positive social behaviors
- Maximum participation—all players have unrestricted opportunities to use required game skills

From Mary and Jose's discussion, it is clear that their second-grade games did not meet the educational games' criteria. One wonders what purpose the games served. And why they were played at all!

What Makes a Game Cooperative?

A cooperative game is an educational game that results in fun, acceptance, and involvement, and requires all players to work together to achieve the goal of the game; the potential for many students to be positively affected is great.

Games Education: Best Practices

As games continue to be used extensively in the preschool through middle school curriculum, it is important that teachers study the following guidelines. If followed, these standards will enable teachers to plan and conduct game experiences that realize the potential benefits of game participation. The following practices reflect a partial listing of components as noted in the 1992 NASPE document, *Developmentally Appropriate Physical Education Practices for Children: A Position Statement of the National Association for Sport and Physical Education/Developed by the Council on Physical Education for Children.*

1. Games are selected, designed, sequenced, and modified by teachers and/or children to maximize the learning and enjoyment of children (Component: Games).

2. Teachers and/or children modify official rules, regulations, equipment, and playing space of adult sports to match the varying abilities of the children (Component: Rules Governing Game Play).

3. Teams are formed in ways that preserve the dignity and self-respect of every child (Component: Forming Teams).

4. Children participate in team games (i.e., two to three per team), which allows for numerous practice opportunities while also allowing children to learn about the various aspects of the game being taught (Component: Number of Children on a Team).

5. Activities emphasize self-improvement, participation, and cooperation instead of winning and losing (Component: Competition).

6. Teachers intentionally design and teach activities throughout the year that allow children the opportunity to work together for the purpose of improving their emerging social and cooperation skills (Component: Affective Development).

7. Children are given the opportunity to practice skills at high rates of success adjusted for their individual skill levels (Component: Success Rate).

8. Enough equipment is available so that each child benefits from maximum participation (Component: Equipment).

9. All children are involved in activities that allow them to remain continuously active (Component: Active Participation for Every Child).

Cooperative Learning Activities
for the Games Education Program

Sportball Juggle

Activity Challenge: To successfully move a maximum number of different sportballs in sequence within a team of five players

Description: Five students standing approximately 12 feet apart in a star pattern attempt to move sportballs simultaneously around the star pattern. Students decide on the types of skills and balls and different levels for each ball. For example, bounce a basketball at a medium height, kick a soccer ball low, set a volleyball high, pass a football straight, roll a bowling ball low, and underhand toss a softball low. The group begins with one ball and adds a ball after the group can successfully move the preceding ball or balls three times around the star.

Equipment: One basketball, volleyball, football, softball, bowling ball and soccer ball for each group of five

Psychomotor Goals: Refine manipulative skills
Extend effort awareness

Cognitive Goal: Improve concentration skills

Affective Goal: Use positive interactions to verbally and physically help and support teammates

Variations: To vary Sportball Juggle, reduce or increase the distance between players, use balls of varying size and texture, or determine how many times a specified number of balls are passed around the star pattern.

Cooperative Learning Structure: Pairs-Check-Perform (Teachers can use several different structures for game skill and strategy instruction, including Think-Share-Perform, Co-op Play, Collective Score, and Jigsaw Perform.)

Slalom Blindfold

I

Activity Challenge: To negotiate a course of cones as fast as possible with the assistance of teammates

Description: In a team of four students, three students tap wands on the floor, attempting to guide a blindfolded teammate through a slalom course of five cones. This course is 30 feet long with five cones spaced five feet apart. Tapping students should tap wands in unison and close together to provide a clear "sound pathway" for the blindfolded player. After practice, teams can work toward moving the blindfolded player quickly through the slalom course. Rotate positions so all players have turns in each game role.

Equipment: Five cones, wand, and a blindfold for each team

Psychomotor Goals: Refine body and spatial awareness

Cognitive Goals: Enhance concentration skills
Enhance problem solving skills

Affective Goal: Use positive interactions to plan and guide teammates

Variations: To vary this activity, change the cone arrangement for slalom course, use obstacles of varying size and shape for slalom course, blindfolded partners.

Cooperative Learning Structure: Co-op Play

Ouch Person

(*Note*: This is a game that is not purely cooperative, but does promote development of affective behaviors and is thoroughly enjoyed by young children.)

Activity Challenge: To either avoid being tagged by the Ouch Person or free tagged players

Description: There are three player roles for this game:

1. Ouch Person—player attempting to tag (i.e., ouch) the target players

2. Target Players—players trying to avoid being tagged by the Ouch Person. If Target Players are tagged, they must stand where they were ouched, holding the ouched body part and shouting, "HELP!"

3. Helper Players—players placing bandages (i.e., piece of masking tape) on the ouch of the tagged player, who is then free to continue running from the Ouch Person. Switch participants so all have the chance to be Target and Helper Players.

Equipment: A "funny" hat or shirt to identify the Ouch Person, pinnies for identifying the Target Players, and 10 to 20 4-inch pieces of masking tape for each Helper Player

Psychomotor Goals: To enhance spatial awareness
                               To promote cardiovascular endurance

Cognitive Goal: To stimulate problem solving skills

Affective Goal: To use positive interactions to help with avoiding and tagging skills

Variations: Increasing the size of the play space should result in greater demands on the cardiovascular system while decreasing the size of the play space requires more thinking and use of spatial awareness. Target and Helper Players could move in connected groups of two or three. Additional Ouch Persons could also be used.

21 Wall Ball

Activity Challenge: To keep a ball in play and remain as close as possible to 21 points

Description: Players numbered 1, 2, 3, and 4 hand strike a small rubber ball so it contacts a front wall, stays inside the playing court, and rebounds one time.

Players, in numbered order, take turns striking the ball. Play begins with #1 and continues in sequence with #2, #3, and #4. After the ball is struck by #4 the sequence repeats. Play begins with 21 points. Each time a ball leaves the playing court, does not contact the front wall, or rebounds more than one time before being struck, the team's score is reduced by one point. A point is also deducted when players hit the ball out of order. Each team can set a goal of how many points can be maintained in how many minutes. For example, after five minutes a team will have 15 points.

Equipment: A small rubber ball and a playing court with a front wall and dimensions of approximately 20 feet wide by 35 feet long

Psychomotor Goals: To refine manipulative skills
To enhance effort awareness skills

Cognitive Goal: To understand ball trajectory

Affective Goal: To use positive interactions to help teammates perform game skills with more skill

Variations: After students can achieve their group goal, the game can be made more difficult by incorporating any or all of the following, depending on the players' proficiency:
- Increase difficulty of group goal.
- Decrease the size of the playing court.
- Decrease the size of the ball.
- Use a paddle instead of hand for striking.

If students are experiencing difficulty achieving their group goal, ask:
- Is the goal realistic?
- Is the size of the playing court, number of players on the team, or the size of the ball harming performance? If so, make appropriate changes.
- Would another player joining the team to model and teach benefit the group?
- Do players demonstrate the appropriate skills needed for successful participation in the game? Could a cooperative learning structure be used to help facilitate skill development (e.g., Learning Teams)?

Cooperative Learning Structure: Co-op Play (Teachers could also use Learning Teams and Pairs-Check-Perform.)

Hoopin'

Activity Challenge: To score as many points as possible with a partner by tossing a ball into a hoop

Description: Organize the players into groups of three, with each group having a hula hoop and several small balls. Designate one player as the thrower and the other players as catchers. The thrower stands behind a line and attempts to throw a ball into a hoop that is held by the catchers, who are standing 12 to 15 feet away. At the release of the ball, catchers moves toward the ball in attempt to catch or "hoop" the ball. Each ball caught scores one point. After the first player throws five balls, players switch positions and repeat. Add the total number of balls caught for the team score. Scores for all teams may be added together.

Equipment: One hoop and several small (three to five inch) balls per group

Psychomotor Goals: To improve manipulative skills
To improve effort awareness

Cognitive Goal: To understand the importance of group movement

Affective Goal: To use positive interactions to encourage and support group efforts of throwing and catching balls

Variations: Some variations include using smaller hoops and larger balls and increasing the distance between thrower and catchers. In order to increase the level of cooperation, multiple players could hold the hoop or the players could be required to bounce the ball one, two, or three times before it is caught. Changing the locomotor skill used by the catchers will increase complexity and enjoyment.

Cooperative Learning Structure: Co-op Play (Collective Score could be used if points are kept. Think-Share-Perform could be used for creating new throwing and catching strategies.)

Movin' Together

Activity Challenge: To respond to commands as quickly as possible

Description: Pairs of students holding hands stand at one end of the playing area. Upon command of the directing person, all players work together to move as directed. Commands are based on a thematic approach. For example, commands based on an ocean theme may include

- "Ship"—all run to one end of the play area;
- "Shore"—all run to opposite end of the play area;
- "Fishnet"—all hold hands to create a net;
- "Sardines"—all lie on floor and touch;
- "Wave"—all do "Fishnet" and move bodies up and down;
- "Submarine"—all form a line and, while touching, lift a leg (i.e., up periscope) and hold nose (i.e., dive);
- "Shark"—all form a line and create a large mouth and dorsal fin, then move quickly; and
- "Octopus"—in small groups, students make a body, head, and tentacles, then move slowly.

Equipment: None, unless used as props

Psychomotor Goals: To refine body and spatial awareness

Cognitive Goal: To encourage creativity

Affective Goal: To use positive interactions to support peers' efforts at collective responding

Variations: Always use a variety of themes to spark student interest (e.g., World Series, Spring, Arm and Shoulder Strength). Have students respond to all commands while in small group. Ask students to help you think of additional commands for forming creatures or objects or performing actions. Continue questioning to encourage students to verbalize the characteristics or parts needed for the creation. Encourage students to decide how many students are needed for each part.

Cooperative Learning Structure: Co-op Play (Co-op Co-op Perform and/or Jigsaw Perform could be used when students are creating their own objects or creatures.)

(Orlick 1978)

Bear on the Loose

Activity Challenge: To cooperatively locate and return stuffed bears to a cardboard box

Description: This is a partner game based on a theme of circus bears escaping from their cages. The teacher tells the children a story of how circus bears have escaped from their cages (cardboard boxes), are hiding throughout the circus grounds (stuffed animal bears placed around the play space), and need to be captured (placed in a paper bag) and returned to their cages before feeding time. Pairs of children jointly holding a bear bag move throughout the play space looking for hidden bears. When a bear is found, the children put it in their bag and return it to the bear cage. The game continues until the pairs of children have returned all the bears to the cage.

Equipment: Five to eight stuffed bear animals and one large plastic or strong paper bag for each pair of students

Psychomotor Goals: Refine spatial awareness
Improve locomotor skills

Cognitive Goal: Understand the concept of two people moving as one

Affective Goal: Use positive interactions to work cooperatively with partner to find bag and return bears

Variations: In order to increase the complexity of the game, locomotor skills can be modified. For example, Partner One gallops, while Partner Two skips. One player from each pair could be blindfolded. Small groups can be used, and the theme can be varied by using different objects or animals: For example, the class can "go fishing." The possibilities are limited only by your imagination.

Cooperative Learning Structure: Co-op Play

Taketak Tie

Activity Challenge: To spin a hula hoop so it falls on the ground at the same time as your partner's hoop

Description: Pairs of students, each with a hula hoop, try to spin hoops with the same speed and force so the hoops fall on the ground and stop at the same time (i.e., a tie). Students discuss and practice various strategies in order to increase skill levels. When the students can end their game in a "tie," both students win.

Equipment: One hula hoop for each student

Psychomotor Goal: Refine effort awareness

Cognitive Goals: Understand timing
                     Improve concentration

Affective Goal: Use positive interactions to cooperate with partner to produce equal spinning speed and force

Variations: You can create several variations to increase the difficulty of this game. For example, use different size hoops within a pair, use different objects for spinning (e.g., Frisbees), use different methods for communicating (e.g., no speaking), regularly and randomly rotate partners and spinning equipment, increase the size of the spinning group from two to ten, or have each player spin two objects.

Cooperative Learning Structure: Think-Share-Perform (Pairs-Check-Perform could be used effectively if the spinning groups were comprised of four players.)

(Orlick 1982)

Towel Ball

Activity Challenge: To toss a ball up into the air so it is jointly caught by two students holding a 2- by 4-foot bath towel.

Description: Two students hold the ends of a towel with a 6- to 8-inch ball placed on it. They toss the ball into the air and catch it with the towel.

Equipment: One towel approximately 2- by 4-feet for each two players and a variety of balls of differing size, shape, and texture

Psychomotor Goals: Improve manipulative skills
Refine spatial awareness
Refine effort awareness

Cognitive Goal: Understand force production

Affective Goal: Use positive interaction to cooperate with partner to successfully pass and catch balls with a towel

Variations: When the students can successfully toss and catch the ball 10 times, they may attempt the following Collective Score games:
 1. Toss ball in air; ball bounces on floor and is caught.
 2. Same as #1, but increase number of bounces before ball is caught.
 3. Same as #1 or #2, but players turn a circle before catching.
 4. Toss ball to a wall and catch.
 5. Toss ball to a wall; ball bounces on floor and is caught.
 6. Same as #5, but increase number of bounces.
 7. Toss and catch with another pair of students.
 8. Toss with another pair; ball bounces on floor and is caught.
 9. Same as #8, but increase number of bounces before ball is caught.
 10. Toss and catch with another pair while moving.
 11. Toss and catch with another pair using a net and out of bounds lines.
 12. Play at traditional games, such as volleyball, but use partners tossing and catching a ball with a towel for means of manipulation. ·
 13. Require students to create games that allow maximum participation and positive interdependence.

Cooperative Learning Structure: Co-op Play (Think-Share-Perform and Pairs-Check-Perform for skill development. Collective Score for playing game with points.)

Bump Over

Activity Challenge: To score a maximum number of points by bumping a ball over a net so it can be returned and bumped back

Description: Two small groups of players stand on either side of a net and bump, or pass with the forearm, a volleyball over the net so it can be bumped back to the other group. A point is scored every time a ball is successfully bumped over the net.

Equipment: A soft volleyball, net of appropriate height, and playing space for two small groups

Psychomotor Goals: Refine effort awareness
Refine spatial awareness
Improve manipulative skills

Cognitive Goals: Understand biomechanical (i.e., how the body moves while performing a skill) principles of flexion, extension, and force production and absorption associated with bumping a volleyball

Affective Goal: Use positive interactions to encourage all players' efforts of bumping

Variations: This "game concept" can be used to practice and apply learning in various skill games, such as basketball passing and throwing and softball catching.

Cooperative Learning Structure: Collective Score

References

Grineski, S. 1988. Teaching and learning in physical education for young children. *Journal of Physical Education, Recreation and Dance* 59(5): 91-94.
———. 1989. Effects of cooperative games on the prosocial interactions of young children with and without impairments. Unpublished PhD diss., University of North Dakota.
———. 1991. Promoting success in physical education: Cooperatively structured learning. *PALAESTRA* 7(2): 26-29.
National Association for Sport and Physical Education. 1992. *Developmentally appropriate physical education practices for children: A position statement of the National Association for Sport and Physical Education/Developed by the Council on Physical Education for Children*. Reston, VA: AAHPERD.
Orlick, T. 1978. *The cooperative sports and games book*. New York: Pantheon.
———. 1982. *The second cooperative sports and games book*. New York: Pantheon.

CHAPTER 6

Cooperative Learning: Dance Education

Students enrolled in an Elementary School Physical Education Methods class were asked about their own experiences with dance in physical education. Their memories tell an interesting story.

"We seemed to do dance when the teacher liked dance, not because it was part of a curriculum."

"At our elementary school, we always did the same dance—it was some kind of line dance. We did this dance every year for six years."

"I remember doing a lot of dancing in elementary school. We did folk, square, and some country dancing. It was fun."

"We never did any dance."

"The only time I remember doing lummi sticks or tinikling was in Scouts. We never did this in school."

"Our teacher said if we didn't behave during the square dance unit, then we couldn't play floor hockey."

"After learning about dance and doing different kinds of dance, I feel cheated [by my negative experiences with dance in school]. I am going to include lots of dancing when I teach."

"I remember the teachers making the girls and boys dance together all the time. I don't think I will do this. It seemed to cause a lot of problems, especially in elementary."

"I had no idea that dance in physical education included so many different kinds of activities since my own experience with dance in PE was so limited. Folk dancing, square dancing, country line dancing, using lummi sticks, tinikling, scarves, streamers, and balls. I liked using children's stories, too. The creative dance was new to me. Kids really like it."

These students' comments provide insight about the status of dance in physical education. Although dancing can be a wonderful educational experience, many times it is poorly taught, or not taught at all. It seems odd that such a positive physical activity is regarded so negatively, or even ignored, by some physical education teachers.

The Dance Education Program

Dance is meaningful movement that expresses feelings, stories, or concepts and uses a variety of movement skills to accomplish these ends. Dance can contribute significantly to the total development of the individual (Murray 1976). This development occurs through experiences designed to enhance learning across the psychomotor, cognitive, and affective domains. How well dance promotes development in these domains is directly related to the quantity and quality of dance opportunities offered to students.

The Structured and Unstructured Approaches

Ideally, the dance education program uses both structured and unstructured approaches.

Structured

Structured dance uses sequences of skills and patterns and is usually teacher-directed. Examples of structured dance include, but are not limited to, folk, square, western, and social dances.

Benefits available to students through structured dance include

- acquisition of nonlocomotor skills, locomotor skills, and specific dance skills and patterns;
- development of balance, agility, coordination, and endurance;
- learning dance-related vocabulary;
- understanding sequencing and synchronization of movement to accompaniment, expressing cooperative behaviors; and
- enjoying skillful movement (Gabbard, LeBlanc, and Lowy 1994).

Unstructured

Unstructured dance involves student-directed problem solving with emphasis on creativity and expression. The elements of movement provide the foundation for unstructured dance. Unstructured dance activities are based on ideas of exploration, interpretation, composition, and relaxation, and are centered on a theme. Themes can include any concept or idea that is meaningful to students. Some examples of themes include seasons, transportation, feelings, animals, sporting events, weather and storms, colors, foods, and so on. Benefits associated with unstructured dance include

- development of body, spatial, and effort awareness;
- moving with or without musical accompaniment;
- learning the basic movement vocabulary;
- planning movement sequences;
- experiencing divergent and creative thinking;
- expression of ideas through movement; and
- cooperating with others (Figley, Mitchell, and Wright 1994).

To be truly educational, dance must be more than memorizing steps and patterns, moving to a rock beat, or exercising to music. Dance education must provide opportunities for students and teachers to cooperate, explore, interpret, think, observe, and evaluate (Grineski 1986). Because the potential for quality physical education through student learning in dance is great, dance must be included as an integral and valuable component of the curriculum. Use of cooperative learning in the dance education program enhances an already valuable curricula area. Another benefit of dance education is that it allows teachers another way to integrate physical education learning across the school curriculum. For example, cultural learning, geography, history, mathematics, and writing can all be extended through the use of dance.

A discussion of dance curriculum, teaching methods, and program components is beyond the scope of this book. For a complete description, see Grineski 1986. This 134-page guide is available for a $5.00 printing charge.

An excellent resource for dance music is Wagon Wheel Records, 8549 Edmarn Avenue, Whittier, CA 90605. Most of the musical accompaniments listed in this chapter can be obtained through this company.

Cooperative Learning Activities
for the Dance Education Program

Carousel—A Folk Dance
With Two Pairs

Activity Challenge: To create a new version of an existing dance

Description: For "Carousel"

1. Partners face each other and hold hands in a scattered formation.
2. Part 1: 12 slow step-draw steps (i.e., step apart and close) three stamp steps (i.e., step in place, alternating feet)
   Part 2: 16 fast step-draw steps
3. To create a new version of the dance follow these steps:
   a. Partners individually think of another movement that goes with the music of part 1.
   b. Share ideas with partner.
   c. Collectively decide on new part 1.
   d. Part 2 remains unchanged.
   e. Practice this new dance.
   f. One partner from each pair sits down, while the other partners remain standing. Each standing student chooses a new partner from the sitting students and teaches the new partner his or her new part 1.
   g. Part 2 remains unchanged.
   h. Practice this new dance with this new partner.
   i. New partners individually think of something different that matches with part 2.
   j. Share ideas with partner.
   k. Collectively decide on new part 2.
   l. Exchange partners; incoming dancer teaches their part 2 and the other partner teaches their part 1.
   m. Practice this new dance.

Equipment: Musical selection for "Carousel"

Musical Accompaniment: "Young People's Folk Dance 1041"

Psychomotor Goal: Improve step-draw step

Cognitive Goal: Encourage problem solving

Affective Goals: Use positive interactions in creating and sharing information

Use positive interactions in supporting partner's decision making

Variations: Using Think-Share-Perform can aid students in collectively modifying and creating many folk dances. Some useful dances are

1. "Round and Round the Village" (Folk Craft Records 1191),
2. "Danish Dance of Greeting" (Folk Craft Records 1187),
3. "Kinder Polka" (Folk Craft Records 1187),
4. "Shoemaker's Dance" (Loyd Shaw E-5),
5. "Troika" (Classroom Materials 1160),
6. "Ach Ja" (Loyd Shaw E-2),
7. "Chimes of Dunkirk" (Young People's Folk Dance 1042),
8. "Cshebogar" (Young People's Folk Dance 1042),
9. "Greensleeves" (Loyd Shaw E-11),
10. "Jump Jim Jo" (Young People's Folk Dance 1042),
11. "Skip to My Lou" (Classroom Materials CM 1159),
12. "Bingo" (Loyd Shaw E-13),
13. "La Raspa" (Young People's Folk Dance 1043),
14. "Crested Hen" (Young People's Folk Dance 1042), and
15. "Hopp Mor Anika" (Young People's Folk Dance 1042).

Descriptions of these dances can be found in Grineski 1986.

Cooperative Learning Structure: Think-Share-Perform

Thunderstorm Dance

Activity Challenge: To create and perform a creative dance based on a thunderstorm theme

Description: Follow these steps to create the Thunderstorm Dance:

1. Conduct a class discussion about the elements of a thunderstorm, such as wind, rain, clouds, lightning, thunder, and hail.
2. Assign small groups of students to each element.
3. Each group discusses their element and thinks about what movements might communicate its characteristics to an audience (e.g., running through many pathways at different levels with differing amounts of force to represent wind) and what props would be appropriate (e.g., throwing Frisbees for the wind).
4. Each group practices their portion of the dance.
5. Each group performs their portion of the dance for the rest of the groups.

6. Appropriate groups (e.g., clouds with rain) are connected as practicing continues.
7. Combine all groups for a performance.

Equipment: Whatever props are needed to support each group's creation

Musical Accompaniment: Rosinni's *1812 Overture* or Holst's *The Planets*

Psychomotor Goals: Promote body and spatial awareness

Cognitive Goal: Encourage problem solving

Affective Goals: Use positive interactions to work together through talking, planning, and supporting

Use positive interactions to support the work of others

Variations: Themes can originate from student interest (e.g., space travel), the season (e.g., blizzard) or an upcoming event (e.g., sports tournament).

Cooperative Learning Structure: Co-op Co-op Perform

Telephone Number Dance

I

Activity Challenge: To cooperatively create a group dance based on a seven-digit telephone number

Description: Students are divided into groups of fourteen and given a seven-digit telephone number. Each pair of students within each group receives a telephone number digit and is responsible for creating movement to represent this digit. For example, "3" might be three arm circles. Each pair of students teaches its number movement to the rest of the group. After each group practices performing all seven movements in sequence, they perform their dance for the rest of the class, and the class tries to guess the telephone number.

Equipment: None, unless a group wishes to use props

Psychomotor Goal: Enhance concept and/or skill required of telephone number dance sequence

Cognitive Goal: Promote creativity

Affective Goal: Use positive interactions to support others' efforts of thinking, remembering, and moving

Variations: This activity is easily modified to meet the needs of students regardless of grade level or developmental level. For example, the telephone number could be replaced with numbers such as birth dates, teeth lost, money saved, batting averages, or math facts. This activity could provide another opportunity for physical education to be linked to the school curriculum. Student groups for creating and performing can be adjusted as appropriate.

Cooperative Learning Structure: Jigsaw Perform

(Grineski and Bynum 1988)

Soft Creatures

Activity Challenge: To cooperatively create a dance using "Soft Creatures"

Description: Give pairs of students large or stretchable outer clothes and newspaper or small soft rags. Students stuff the clothes with the newspaper or rags to form a "Soft Creature." Pairs then create a circle dance using their creatures. Encourage students to include the dance movements of circling, arching, all hands to the middle, and swinging.

Equipment: One set of outer clothes and a large bundle of newspaper or soft rags per pair of students

Musical Accompaniment: Hap Palmer, *Creative Music and Rhythmic Expression*, Educational Activities, Inc., Freeport, NY 11520

Psychomotor Goals: Improve body awareness
Improve spatial awareness
Improve dance movements

Cognitive Goal: Enhance creativity

Affective Goal: Use positive interactions to encourage peers' creativity

Variations: After students have created threesome dances, combine groups to make sixsome dances, ninesome dances, and a whole class dance.

Cooperative Learning Structure: Co-op Play (Teachers could also have students use Jigsaw Perform and Co-op Co-op Perform for creating dances.)

Cumberland Square Eight

I

Activity Challenge: To perform the "Cumberland Square Eight" dance correctly

Description: Students form square sets of four couples, designated as head, foot, and side couples. Couples can be opposite-sex partners or same-sex partners. When using same sex partners, have all dancers standing on the right wear a funny tie. There are many ways to create a couple other than by gender.

1. Head and foot couples, facing partners and holding hands, gallop across the set in eight slides with boys passing back to back. Return to home position with eight slides.
2. Repeat action with side couples.
3. Head and foot couples come together in middle of the set, forming a right-hand star (i.e., all touch right hands) for eight counts, then a left-hand star (i.e., all touch left hands) for eight counts and back to place.
4. Repeat action with side couples.
5. Head and foot couples form a basket: Boys join hands with each other behind the girls' backs and the girls extend their hands behind and under the boys' arms and join hands with each other in front of the boys. Circle to the left and then back to place (16 counts).
6. Repeat action with side couples. All join hands and circle to the left (16 counts).
7. Promenade back to home position (16 counts).

Equipment: Musical selection for "Cumberland Square Eight"

Musical Accompaniment: *World of Fun Folk Dance and Games* Record #5. R. Harold Hipps and Wallace E. Chappel, Discipleship Resources, P.O. Box 840, Nashville, TN 37202.

Psychomotor Goals: Refine sliding, buzz swing, star dance movements

Cognitive Goal: Enhance concentration skills

Affective Goal: Use positive interaction to help others learn dance movements

Variations: To make the dance more interesting, the squares could set up four feet behind each other. When the head and foot couples do their eight slides they would cross into the adjacent squares. If the class is big enough, squares could also be added on the sides to produce more crossing over.

Cooperative Learning Structure: Pairs-Check-Perform

Perpetual Motion Machine

I

Activity Challenge: To cooperatively create a perpetual motion machine

Description: Students in groups of four create a sequence of three movements (i.e., movement one by Student One, and so on) with each movement being performed by a different group member. The sequence of three movements represents the machine creating its product, while the fourth member of the group is responsible for pantomiming the machine's product. Students work together on deciding on each individual's movement and the product of the machine. Student One must initiate Student Two's movement, while Student Two's movement must initiate Student Three's movement and so forth. Student Three's movement results in the product. After sufficient practice, the machine becomes "perpetual." Each group can perform their machine with the other groups attempting to guess the machine and its product.

Equipment: None

Musical Accompaniment: The "Move Like a Machine" musical selection from the recording *Perceptual Motor Rhythm Games* by Educational Activities, Inc. (Freeport, NY 11520), works well with this dance.

Psychomotor Goals: Refine nonlocomotor skills
Refine body awareness

Cognitive Goal: Enhance creativity

Affective Goal: Use positive interactions to encourage productive group decision making

Variations: Instead of creating a machine and product, the group could work collaboratively to create and perform an "Advertisement Dance." In this variation, group members receive a product idea (e.g., computer), discuss its characteristics (e.g., hardware, software, low buzzing sound, clicking of keyboard) and create a movement for each characteristic. Following practice, charades can be played.

Cooperative Learning Structure: Co-op Play or Co-op Co-op Perform

Tinikling

Activity Challenge: To perform tinikling skills as a result of belonging to a Learning Team

Background: The actions of the dance represent a long-legged bird walking in tall grass. Tinikling is popular in Southeast Asia.

Description: Students are placed in groups of four, with the following roles: one performer or dancer, one helper, and two strikers or pole movers. The dancer practices the tinikling dance steps while the helper provides visual and/or verbal feedback regarding performance. The strikers manipulate the poles, enabling the dancer to perform the tinikling dance steps. Students rotate through to all roles.

To perform the basic tinikling dance step each group needs two eight-foot bamboo poles. The strikers kneel at each end and hold the poles about 12 inches apart on the floor. The striking pattern is two vertical taps to the floor and one sliding movement of the poles together (i.e., TAP, TAP, TOGETHER). With the dancer standing next to one of the poles, the basic dance step is as follows:

1. Step over pole with right foot and stand IN between poles while the left foot remains OUTSIDE the poles on first vertical tap of pole.
2. Step over pole with left foot and stand IN between poles on second vertical tap of pole.
3. Step OUTside of poles with right foot and stand on right foot, lifting left foot straight UP into the air as poles move together.

The following cue words are used: IN, IN, OUT/UP for the dancer and TAP, TAP, TOGETHER for the striker.

Equipment: Two 8-foot tinikling poles for four students

Psychomotor Goal: Improve locomotor (dance) skills

Cognitive Goal: Refine concentration

Affective Goal: Use positive interactions to teach and encourage group members

Variations: Once students master the basic tinikling step (i.e., IN, IN, OUT/UP), they will enjoy these variations:

1. Jump IN, Jump, Jump OUT.
2. Starting by standing in between poles: Jump, Jump, Jump OUT.
3. Repeat #1 and #2 using hopping skills.
4. Require students to create new patterns.

Cooperative Learning Structure: Learning Teams

Blowin' Balloons

Activity Challenge: To cooperatively role-play a balloon lost in a blizzard

Description: Discuss with students what would happen to a balloon if it was outside during a blizzard. Have students watch as the teacher slowly blows up a balloon (pretend to use a pump while making "shooshing" sounds) and then releases it into the room. Ask for descriptions of the balloon's actions. Try to encourage use of movement words (e.g., fast/slow, rising/sinking). Request that pairs of students make a deflated balloon shape by lying on floor, holding hands, and assuming a tight, round, and curled shape. As the teacher slowly or quickly pumps up the balloons, students rise slowly/quickly and assume a round shape. At 100% inflation, the teacher opens the "window" and lets in the blizzard. Balloons move all over the play space, changing level, direction, pathway, and size before settling on the floor in a deflated state. When students begin to understand inflation, deflation, and balloon movements, increase size of groups. Try setting a goal for creating a balloon dance to include all members of the class, grade level, or school. Use music with a windy and stormy mood to enhance learning and enjoyment.

Equipment: Props always increase interest in a creative dance lesson. Try balloons, bicycle pump, and appropriate musical selections.

Psychomotor Goals: Improve spatial awareness
Improve effort awareness

Cognitive Goal: Enhance concentration skills

Affective Goal: Use positive interactions to encourage and support group moving in unison

Variations: Activity idea can be used for any creative dance theme.

Cooperative Learning Structure: Co-op Play

Dancin' and Movin'

P

Activity Challenge: To cooperatively and correctly respond to dance calls

Description: Students start in groups of two, and then change to groups of four or eight depending on the dance calls centered on a theme, such as the Wild West:

1. "Hit the Trail"—Run as fast as possible with partner.
2. "Stop and Keep Time"—Stand still and clap with partner to a beat.
3. "Tornado"—Join hands in a foursome and spin.
4. "Tumbleweed"—Log roll with partner.
5. "Swing Your Partner"—Elbow swing partner.
6. "Circle Right/Left"—Groups of eight form a circle and move in appropriate direction.
7. "Wild Horse"—Groups of four hold hands and slide.
8. "Buffalo Stampede"—All join hands and run in place stomping loudly.
9. "Deliver the Mail"—With hands joined, partners shake hands with other groups of two.
10. "Wagon Wheel"—All lie on floor while touching.

Equipment: None

Musical Accompaniment: Appropriate music that matches theme and enhances learning and enjoyment. For example, Hap Palmer, *Creative Movement and Rhythmic Expression*, Educational Activities, Inc. (Freeport, NY 11520), or "Cotton Eye Joe," Folk Craft 1035.

Psychomotor Goals: Improve locomotor (dance) skills
Improve spatial awareness
Improve body awareness
Improve effort awareness

Cognitive Goal: Improve memory skills

Affective Goal: Use positive interactions to facilitate moving in unison

Variations: Teachers can have students use any theme, skill, and movement in this dance activity. Allow students to create their own themes and decide on skills and movements.

Cooperative Learning Structure: Co-op Play or Co-op Co-op Perform

Body Parts Aerobics

$\boxed{I}$

Activity Challenge: To cooperatively create an aerobic routine using specified body parts

Description: Students in groups of six are instructed to create an aerobic routine that matches a musical selection, uses specified body parts, and results in elevated heart rates. For example, three arms, one neck, and four to six feet used in movement for eight minutes. Give students time to design and practice aerobic movements and match movements to music. Musical selections should have a moderate tempo and steady beat. Pairs of students within the group should be responsible for creating and teaching specific body part movements to other group members.

Equipment: Choices of ropes, balls, hoops, scooters, and musical selections for use in routines

Psychomotor Goals: Enhance cardiovascular endurance
Improve muscular strength

Cognitive Goal: Enhance decision making

Affective Goal: Use positive interactions to create routines and support aerobic workout

Variations: Students can use any combination of body parts or body movement.

Cooperative Learning Structure: Jigsaw Perform

References

Figley, G., H. Mitchell, and B. Wright. 1994. *Elementary school physical education: An educational experience.* 2d ed. Dubuque, IA: Kendall/Hunt.

Gabbard, C., B. LeBlanc, and S. Lowy. 1994. *Physical education for children: Building the foundation.* 2d ed. Englewood Cliffs, NJ: Prentice-Hall.

Grineski, S. 1986. *Dance: A resource guide K-12: North Dakota Arts Curriculum Project.* Bismarck, ND: North Dakota Department of Public Instruction.

———. 1991. Creative dance: A curriculum priority. *Teaching Elementary Physical Education* 2(2): 11-13.

Grineski, S. and R. Bynum. 1988. Creative problem solving in dance. *Journal of Physical Education, Recreation and Dance* 59(4): 12.

Iowa State Department of Education. 1986. *Dance: A guide to curriculum development in the arts.* Des Moines: Iowa State Department of Public Instruction.

Murray, R. 1976. A statement of belief. In *Children's dance*, edited by G. Fleming, 5. Reston, VA: American Alliance for Health, Physical Education, Recreation and Dance.

CHAPTER 7

Cooperative Learning: Gymnastic Education

Many children enjoy gymnastics because of its play-like nature: swinging, climbing, rolling, balancing, hanging upside down, and supporting one's body weight. Gymnastics in the preschool through middle school curriculum should have an educational rather than performance or competitive focus. Teachers should create a program that emphasizes challenging activities and encourages appropriate and safe risk taking. The program should be skill-driven and designed to accommodate for developmental differences.

Enhancing Goals Through Learning in Gymnastics

Many instructional goals can be approached through gymnastics. Some body, spatial, and effort awareness goals include

- identifying body parts;
- demonstrating an awareness of body shapes and body movement;
- using different body parts for support;
- moving with a partner;
- understanding boundaries associated with self space;
- moving the body in different levels, directions, and pathways;
- monitoring body position while performing group stunts and demonstrating movement combinations;
- enhancing strength; and
- enhancing flexibility.

The cognitive and affective goals of quality physical education are also achieved through an educational gymnastic program that uses cooperative learning.

Before a teacher begins lessons in the area of gymnastics, the following safety procedures should be addressed:

1. Precede vigorous activity with warm-up movements that focus on muscle groups to be used in activity.
2. Always teach in a sequential manner.
3. Learn to anticipate problems—think ahead.
4. Instruct students about the benefits and potential risks associated with gymnastics.
5. Teach students that spotting means assisting, not interfering.
6. Encourage students to support others' efforts.
7. Always use quality mats for any gymnastic activity.

Cooperative Learning Activities
for the Gymnastic Education Program

Routines: "Let's Do It Together"

Activity Challenges: To cooperatively create and perform floor routines

Description: Following instruction on basic tumbling skills and stunts, small groups of three students make skill/movement cards for creating routines to perform for the rest of the class. Each 3- by 5-inch card should have symbols representing a skill or movement for use in a routine. For example, — could represent straight line rolling, while *** could represent a curled body shape. The teacher should check that the skills and movements include all of the tumbling and balancing skills the students have learned, in addition to including all movement concepts. Divide the routine cards equally among pairs of students, making each pair responsible for creating a portion of the routine. Once you create each portion of the routine, teach each pair and combine into a whole routine to be performed by the class.

When students are involved in this activity, provide each group with their own work space and necessary materials to accomplish this task. Circulate regularly and ask students questions to check for understanding, hold them accountable, keep them on-task, and help you anticipate any problem.

Equipment: Ten 3- by 5-inch cards for each group, marking pencils, mats, and any appropriate equipment for each pair of students

Psychomotor Goals: Develop and refine tumbling skills

Cognitive Goal: Enhance problem solving

Affective Goal: Use positive interactions to teach other students routines

Cooperative Learning Structure: Jigsaw Perform

A Progression for Learning a Tumbling Skill: Cartwheel

P

Activity Challenge: To perform the cartwheel correctly and help others do so

Description: Three sequential activities are used to learn the cartwheel:

A. Teacher describes and demonstrates "Jumping Over the Creek":

   Stand on one side of a strip of blue paper (i.e., the creek) and place hands on the other side. While in this stretched position, jump over the creek so as not to get feet wet. As the creek rises and widens, jump higher to keep feet dry.

B. Teacher describes and demonstrates "I'm a Little Teapot":

   Stand with hands outstretched over head. On command of "Tip the Pot" bend sideways at the waist and place hands on floor. When hands touch the floor, "Pour the Tea" by jumping sideways and landing on two feet. Progress to landing one foot at a time.

C. Teacher describes and demonstrates "Hand-Hand-Foot-Foot":

   Standing with hands outstretched, place lead hand, then other hand, on the floor and lift back leg off floor. While in this position, lift front leg off the floor and assume a temporary hand stand position. With elbows straight, place back leg, then front leg on floor and return to an upright position.

   Following instruction by the teacher, students are placed in groups of four (two pairs) for skill practice. They follow these steps to practice each skill:

   1. In each pair, Student One practices the skill, while Student Two provides encouragement and help.
   2. When Student One can perform correctly, this person becomes the encourager/helper and Student Two becomes the performer.
   3. When both students in each pair have performed correctly, they join together with the other pair in their foursome and all four students perform. If all students agree that performances were correct, the pairs begin with the next cartwheel activity. If there is disagreement, students continue practicing until all are in agreement.

Equipment: Tumbling mats and materials to make a "blue creek"

Psychomotor Goal: Acquire the cartwheel skill

Cognitive Goal: Understand weight transfer

Affective Goal: Use positive interactions to encourage and help fellow students

Variations: This cooperative learning structure can be effective for skill acquisition in many gymnastic skills, including the shoulder roll, forward roll, backward roll, and round-off.

Cooperative Learning Structure: Pairs-Check-Perform (Learning Teams could also be used with this content.)

Cooperative Tumbling Stunts

P

Activity Challenge: To perform tumbling stunts cooperatively

Description:

1. "Twister"—Two children stand, face each other, and shake right hands. Student One swings right leg over the head of Student Two and takes a straddle position, then Student Two swings left leg over Student One and takes a straddle position. Players reverse process to assume original hand shake position.

2. "Threesome Jump"—Three children hold hands in a circle. With Student One and Student Two lifting, Student Three jumps over the joined hands of Student One and Student Two. Try having Student Three jump back to original starting position.

3. "Partner Handstand Walk"—Two children stand and face each other with Student One placing hands on top of feet of Student Two. On command of "GO," Student One kicks to a handstand with Student Two firmly grasping the ankles. Partners balance, then cooperatively walk.

4. "Lift It Up!"—Two children stand, face each other, and place palms of hands together. On command of "GO," both children slowly move feet away from partner's feet as far as possible without bridge collapsing. Return to upright position.

5. "Partner Bouncing"—Two children stand facing each other and extend left legs so partner can grasp this ankle. Partners balance, then cooperatively hop without falling.

6. "Maximum Coffee Grinder"—Two children, each with one hand supporting their extended body and feet touching the floor, walk feet in a circle, pivoting on the support hand. Children keep support hands as close as possible to each other without touching. Add more players when previous grouping can perform for 15 seconds without contact.

7. "Wring the Dishrag"—Two children stand, face each other, and hold hands. On command of "GO," children turn under an arch formed by their joined hands. Encourage partners to move in unison, perhaps in keeping time to music with an even tempo.

8. "Partner Rolling"—Two students lie in an extended position and, while holding hands, perform a log roll without letting go of hands. Repeat, but try joining feet together. Challenge students to roll in groups of three, four, or more players.

Equipment: Mats and spotters, other items as noted in each description

Psychomotor Goals: Develop body awareness
Improve arm/shoulder strength
Improve flexibility

Cognitive Goal: Understand importance of balancing and moving together

Affective Goal: Use positive interactions to help others perform stunts

Variations: Request that students create their own stunts based on the eight stunts listed.

Cooperative Learning Structure: Co-op Play (Pairs-Check-Perform can be used effectively with partner stunts.)

Cooperative Balances

Activity Challenge: To perform balance positions cooperatively

Description:

1. "Sitting Balance"—The base person lies on mat with knees bent and feet up. A partner sits on the feet of the base while facing the base and holds her hands. The base person tries to work toward straightening her legs while top person uses hands to maintain balance.

2. "Horizontal Stand"—The base person lies on mat with knees bent, feet on floor, and arms extended straight toward the ceiling. The partner places hands on base's knees with his or her elbows slightly bent and puts ankles up to be held by the base. Both the top and base should work toward straightening elbows as far as they will extend.

3. "Group Single-Knee Balance"—In groups of four or eight, students assume a single-knee balance position with all hands held to form a circle. The group should try to maintain balance position for a specific time.

4. "Double Top"—Two students stand as close as possible to one another with feet touching, facing each other and holding hands. In this position, they lean away from each other until arms are fully extended. They move slowly in a circle while maintaining the extended arm and feet together position. Try to increase speed and/or number of students in the group.

5. "Centipede"—The base person places hands and knees on floor. The first segment person places hands two feet in front of the base and legs and trunk on the base. A comfortable position should be arranged between these persons. To move, the base raises off the knees and walks with feet and hands, while the segment person moves arms. After comfortable positioning occurs add additional segment persons. Try to have a maximum number of persons move a maximum distance.

6. "Push-Me-Pull-Me"—Three students stand one behind the other close together. On command, the first two sit on the knees of the student directly behind them. Another group of three students facing the original group of three students performs the same task. When all students are sitting, the two front students join hands. Now, this grouping becomes a "Push-Me-Pull-Me." The group can go in either direction—with one group moving forward and one group moving backward.

7. "Balance Cards"—After students have had ample opportunity to create balance positions that solve all the challenges, allow students to create their own balance routines. Create a "Balance Card Box" by placing numerous 3- by 5-inch cards with various balance words into a shoe box. Groups of students select four cards and, based on the card information, create a balance position. Balance words can include the following: low, medium, high levels; straight, curled, stretched, twisted shapes; self and general space; back, front, side lying; and various body parts.

8. "Group Wheelbarrow"—The base person holds onto the lower legs of two wheelbarrow positioned students. Wheelbarrow students can either face the same or opposite directions. Ask students if they can create a wheelbarrow with more than three people. The group should move in as many directions as possible with varying speeds.

9. "Creative Balance Positions"—In groups of three to five, students create a balance position based on the challenges you provide.

Groups balance with

1. persons at a low, medium, and high level;
2. all feet and all hands touching;
3. the base of support changing;
4. four different body parts on the floor;
5. taking up lots of space;
6. taking up only a little space;
7. taking the shapes of letters O, M, T, N, D;
8. making curled and straight shapes;
9. making twisted shapes; and
10. making at least three right angles.

Equipment: Mats for all balance work

Psychomotor Goals: Improve static balance
                        Improve dynamic balance

Cognitive Goal: Understand balance in relation to others

Affective Goal: Use positive interactions to design effective balance routines

Variations: To continue challenging the group, you can increase group size, blindfold or restrict movement of students, or require students to move in and out of balanced positions using smooth transitions. For example, individual students could slide toward group members, perform a balance position, and then roll away from group members at the completion of the balance position.

Cooperative Learning Structure: Co-op Play

CHAPTER 8

Cooperative Learning: Physical Fitness Education

Physical fitness education is an integral part of the physical education program and includes physical training, concept understanding, and appreciation for and enjoyment of participation in physical activity. The focus of this training, understanding, and appreciation is on health-related and skill-related areas. Health-related concerns, which center on what affects long-term health and wellness, include cardiovascular endurance, flexibility, body composition, and muscular strength and endurance. The skill-related areas, including balance, agility, coordination, speed, and power, are linked to motor performance in games and sport. This holistic approach has great potential to affect the lives of students positively.

Best Practices in Physical Fitness Education

Instructional decisions made by teachers greatly influence the quality of physical fitness education experienced by students. Given the health risks that result from minimal physical activity, as well as the lack of understanding of and negative attitudes about participation, it is critical for teachers to plan and conduct programs that challenge, encourage, and reinforce students' efforts to become and remain physically fit.

The following are practices that can positively affect teaching and learning in physical fitness education programs:

- Physical fitness teaching should be an integral part of the physical education curriculum.
- Physical fitness testing should provide information about the health and fitness of a student, not about how he compares to the physical performances of others.
- Physical fitness training should challenge each student at her level of fitness and not be an experience in predetermined failure.
- Learning in physical fitness should address important concepts related to physical training and healthy living.
- Students should learn that ideas like "no pain no gain" and "more is better" are contraindicated for persons trying to achieve appropriate levels of physical fitness.
- Physical fitness learning should be physically and psychologically safe and enjoyable for all students.
- Use of cooperative small groups can provide support and encouragement for students while they are participating in vigorous activity.

Goals Associated With Physical Fitness Education

The overall aim of fitness education is for students to make lifestyle decisions that will positively affect their health. In order for students to be informed decision-makers, learning experiences in physical fitness must be goal-directed across the three domains of learning: psychomotor, cognitive, and affective. The following are appropriate goals or outcomes that relate to the development of physical fitness. These goals are from the NASPE (1991) document on physical education outcomes. For a complete listing see the NASPE document.

Psychomotor Goals
1. Maintain continuous aerobic activity for a specific time.
2. Monitor heart rate before, during, and after activity.
3. Correctly demonstrate activities designed to improve and maintain muscular strength and endurance, flexibility, and cardiovascular functioning.

Cognitive Goals
1. Describe healthful benefits that result from regular and appropriate participation in physical activity.
2. Identify principles of training and conditioning for physical activity.

Affective Goals

1. Enjoy participation in physical activities alone and with others.
2. Celebrate personal successes and achievements and those of others.
3. Enjoy feelings that result from involvement in physical activity.

Teachers who work toward developing physically fit students face a great and important challenge. By using cooperative structures, teachers can help students enjoy regular participation in vigorous physical activity, understand the body of knowledge that supports this participation, and encourage the efforts of others.

Cooperative Learning Activities
for the Physical Fitness Education Program

Collective Score Exercises

Activity Challenge: To collectively perform as many exercises as possible in a given time

Description: Students in groups of four perform as many exercise repetitions as possible in a given time and add the repetitions for a collective score. After a brief rest period, each group sets a target goal for the number of repetitions they think they can accomplish. Each group's target goal is added together to make a class goal. Students perform and add scores together to determine if they achieved their class goal. Appropriate exercises include push-ups, sit-ups, jumping jacks, pull-ups, rope skipping, vertical or horizontal jumps, running in place, dips, crab walk position, arm circles, crab walk position kicks, hopping, and jumping off and on short boxes.

Equipment: None

Psychomotor Goals: Develop strength and endurance

Cognitive Goals: Reinforce remembering and counting skills

Affective Goal: Use positive interactions to encourage team members to work hard

Variations: Students not able to perform the exercise during the entire time limit continue to count seconds as they hold the isometric position of the exercise (e.g., maintain the push-up position). Scores can be added together to determine a grade-level score or a school score.

Cooperative Learning Structure: Collective Score

Scoop 'Em Up

Activity Challenge: To return as many balls as possible in the allotted time

Description: Students, holding hands in pairs, with one student holding a scoop, run through the play space and scoop up scattered yarn balls. Students return yarn balls to boxes that are located near the center of the play space. Groups attempt to return all yarn balls to the boxes as fast as possible. Prior to beginning the activity, each member of the twosome should think about strategies for quickly scooping and returning yarn balls. Students share these strategies with each other, decide which strategies to use and when to use the selected strategies, and then play.

Equipment: One scoop per group of players and as many yarn balls or small, soft balls as possible

Psychomotor Goal: Improve cardiovascular endurance

Cognitive Goal: Enhance decision making

Affective Goal: Use positive interactions to work together in planning and moving in unison

Variations: Increasing group size and changing locomotor skill are two methods for increasing difficulty in Scoop 'Em Up."

Cooperative Learning Structure: Think-Share-Perform

Challenges

I

Activity Challenge: To correctly solve fitness challenges

Description: Teacher identifies a physical fitness challenge, including the

1. number of seconds or repetitions (e.g., 30 seconds),
2. fitness component to be addressed (e.g., strength or endurance), and
3. equipment needed (e.g., folded tumbling mat).

Pairs of students solve the challenge by sharing their ideas with one another, deciding on collective solutions, and then trying out the solutions to determine which solution is most acceptable. An example of a solution to the example challenge is children pushing a mat around the play space for 30 seconds, or jumping on a lower mat for 30 seconds.

Equipment: Four different challenge cards per pair and whatever equipment is required to solve the challenge (in the example, a foldable tumbling mat)

Psychomotor Goal: Improve specified fitness component of the challenge

Cognitive Goals: Enhance decision making and conflict resolution

Affective Goal: Use positive interactions to plan and perform the fitness challenge

Variations: Allow students to create their own physical fitness challenges. Increase the size of the group.

Cooperative Learning Structure: Think-Share-Perform

Help Me Up Sit-Ups

P

Activity Challenge: To perform as many sit-ups as possible by collectively sitting up and pulling on a parachute

Description: Students in a large group sit with their legs under a stretched out parachute and, using an overhand grip, perform sit-ups by collectively pulling on the chute. When first performing these sit-ups, the teacher could give students a cue to allow the group to move in unison, for example, starting on backs "Up," then "Down." Each student's pulling action assists students located on the other side of the chute to sit up. Students can be encouraged to set a goal of how many sit-ups might be done in a predetermined time.

Equipment: A parachute large enough for each student in a class to have room to sit under and hold

Psychomotor Goal: Develop abdominal strength

Cognitive Goal: Understand idea of moving in unison with others

Affective Goals: Use positive interactions to encourage other students to sit up and pull in unison with others

Use positive interactions to support the physical efforts of others

Cooperative Learning Structure: Collective Score

Cooperative Touch and Go   P I

Activity Challenge: To collectively touch as many beanbags as possible

Description: Students in pairs and holding hands run through the play space and touch as many scattered beanbags as possible. Each bean-bag touched by the pair scores one point. A touch equals all four hands of the pair contacting the bag. Students may not move bags. Points are accumulated by pairs, then added for a group total. A time limit may be set for a specific number of points to be scored by the group.

Equipment: 50 to 75 bean bags for a class of 30 students

Psychomotor Goals: Develop cardiovascular endurance
                                Refine spatial awareness

Cognitive Goal: Stimulate problem solving

Affective Goal: Use positive interactions to encourage partner and other pairs to move quickly and touch as many beanbags as possible

Variations: To extend cooperation and problem solving
- have three or more students hold hands;
- require players to use specific body parts for contact with team members;
- limit communication style for players (i.e., some players may only speak, others only see, and others do not speak or see); and
- require some players to use a different locomotor skill than other team members.

Intermediate grade players may enjoy these variations.

Cooperative Learning Structure: Collective Score

Pushin' Through the Maze

P I

Activity Challenge: To collectively push a stack of tumbling mats through a maze made of various pathways

Description: Students in groups of four attempt to push one to three stacked tumbling mats through various pathways in a predetermined time. The pathways should include curved as well as straight lines and use narrow and wide borders. The pushing position is with the head up, hands on the long edge of the mat, and knees off the ground while running.

Equipment: One to three folded tumbling mats per group of three students and cones to mark pathways and borders

Psychomotor Goals: Develop cardiovascular endurance
Develop muscular strength

Cognitive Goals: Enhance problem solving skills
Enhance negotiation skills

Affective Goal: Use positive interactions to encourage and support efforts directed at collective mat pushing

Variations: Imposing a mean time goal for all groups, adding mats or some type of weight on the stacked mats, and requiring groups to use a gallop, hop, or jump for locomotion are three variations for the activity. Intermediate grade players may enjoy using a sophisticated maze.

Cooperative Learning Structure: Co-op Play (Collective Score could be used when time is kept, while Think-Share-Perform would be appropriate for developing strategies.)

Shadow Running

Activity Challenge: To move through the play space for a specific time while maintaining arm's-length distance

Description: Students in pairs standing one in front of the other move through the play space while attempting to maintain an arm's-length distance without touching one another. Pairs can move through the play space during a musical selection and stop when the music stops. After players have practiced sufficiently, teacher can monitor pairs for appropriate arm's-length spacing. This can be accomplished with random checks while students are moving or stopped. If you wish, try using a system for scoring points. A point can be scored or deducted for maintaining or not maintaining an arm's-length distance.

Teachers can use either a left to right scan observation technique or a five-second-interval observation technique for a specific area of the play space for observing and counting points.

The purpose of the activity is to promote fitness through cooperation, not to be 100% accurate on point counting.

Equipment: None

Psychomotor Goal: Enhance cardiovascular endurance

Cognitive Goal: Enhance concentration skills

Affective Goal: Use positive interactions to support player efforts at maintaining arm's-length distance and running for distance

Variations: To vary this activity, have more than two students run in tandem; modify the distance between runners, locomotor skill, running course, or pathways; or change the length of time for running. Intermediate level students may enjoy these variations.

Cooperative Learning Structure: Co-op Play (Collective Score if points are scored.)

Student-Created Obstacle Courses

Activity Challenge: To create an obstacle course and th
lectively through the course as fast as possible

Description: Using Jigsaw Perform, students are instructed t
an obstacle course. Small groups of students are responsible for e.
portion of the obstacle course. Each group must use the equipment
and space provided and create an obstacle; the way of negotiating (e.g.,
locomotor skill, using a scooter board) each obstacle, however, may be
determined by the teacher. After five minutes, each group shows the
other groups how to perform their obstacle. After this demonstration,
students are placed in groups that are different from their obstacle-
making group. This arrangement provides several "experts" to help
when moving through specific obstacles. The students then hold onto
a small rope and negotiate the course of obstacles. Groups are instructed
to move as quickly as possible, and to avoid touching any of the obstacles. If an obstacle is wrecked or disturbed, the group must return it
to its original position before continuing. A timed and contact score
may be taken. The timed score would be the time for completing the
course, while the contact time would be adding time for contacting
obstacles or subtracting time for not contacting obstacles.

Equipment: Appropriate equipment for the obstacle course

Psychomotor Goals: Develop arm, shoulder, and leg strength
Enhance cardiovascular endurance

Cognitive Goals: Promote creativity and problem solving skills

Affective Goal: Use positive interactions to help other students decide on effective ways to negotiate obstacles

Variations: Changing the pathways of the course, the size of the groups,
and the locomotor skills, direction, and level used to move through
pathways are appropriate variations.

Cooperative Learning Structure: Jigsaw Perform (Collective Score
is appropriate when scoring points.)

artner Straddle Stretch

P

Activity Challenge: To stretch the muscle groups of the low back and leg with a partner

Description: Partners of similar height straddle sit on the floor in a back-to-back position. Partner One leans slowly backward, gently pushing Partner Two toward the floor. When Partner Two feels a slight "tugging" in the low back and/or legs, he tells Partner One to stop and then holds this position for three to five seconds. After this holding, Partner One leans slowly forward to the original starting position. Repeat steps with Partner Two leaning and Partner One being stretched.

Equipment: None, but use of music with a slow tempo may enhance slow stretching (e.g., Hap Palmer, "Movin'," Educational Activities, Inc., Freeport, NY 11520)

Psychomotor Goal: Improve flexibility in low back and leg muscle groups

Cognitive Goal: Understand the importance of stretching slowly

Affective Goal: Use positive interactions to carefully stretch partner

Variation: Alternate partner groupings.

Cooperative Learning Structure: Co-op Play

Crazy Hoopin' Lines

Activity Challenge: To pass a maximum number of hoops down a curved line made by students who are holding hands

Description: Students holding hands and standing in curved lines of 12 to 20 students pass hula hoops from one end of the line to the other. During hoop passing, students must keep hands held, and maintain their original curved pathway and body position. Pathways must have at least three curves. Students' body positions must include alternating low, medium, and high levels. Have students work toward passing a maximum number of hoops as quickly and as slowly as possible.

Equipment: 30 to 50 hoops per 15 students

Psychomotor Goal: Improve flexibility

Cognitive Goals: Understand the concepts of flexion, extension, and rotation

Affective Goal: Use positive interactions to assist other line players in hoop passing

Variations: Performing the activity with eyes closed, with no talking, while standing on one foot, while balancing on a line or while jumping continuously are a few variations. If scoring is desired, students could be awarded points for the number of hoops passed in a specified time. Scores could then be added for a collective score.

Cooperative Learning Structure: Co-op Play (Collective Score if points are kept.)

References

Grineski, S. 1994. Cooperative fitness activities. *Teaching Elementary Physical Education* 5(1): 14-15.

National Association for Sport and Physical Education (NASPE). 1992. *Outcomes of quality physical education programs.* Reston, VA: American Alliance for Health, Physical Education, Recreation and Dance.

CHAPTER 9

Social Inertia and Change: What's Next for Physical Education?

What does the future hold for preschool, elementary, and middle school physical education? A look at our history can help us think about this question.

A Look at the Past and Today

Many times early childhood through middle school physical education programs have been characterized by common but questionable practices. These practices include curricula that lack content variety and that focus on large group competitive activities offering minimal opportunities for skill development. Another common problem is that curriculum choices reflect interests of the teacher, rather than needs of the students. For example, some programs have little or no coverage of dance, relying heavily on competitive relays and games. In addition, many programs ignore both the developmental differences of same-age students and the development of positive social behavior, although such development is viewed as an important physical education outcome. The main reason for these deficiencies has been excessive use of individual and competitive learning activities with little or no cooperative learning opportunities for students. The result is that many adults have negative memories about physical education, and so they fail to support the continuation or growth of programs.

INSIGHTS FROM THE GYM

When adults were asked to describe memories of their experiences in physical education, they shared the following:

"If you can picture the football coach with a whistle around his neck running P.E. class, you can see what my experience was like. It was really bad."

"I hated the elimination games. I always felt terrible when I was knocked out."

"Others got hurt when we played dodgeball with those big, red balls."

"I wasn't a great athlete, sort of mediocre, so I fit into the middle."

"Physical education was a break from real school."

"My teacher was not knowledgeable enough to address the cognitive domain."

"Gym was pretty much a slough hour."

"Physical education did not give me better skills to draw upon later . . . I learned them elsewhere."

Some readers might assume that these statements are not representative of most physical education programs. The National Children and Youth Fitness Studies I (Ross et al. 1985) and II (Ross et al. 1987), Placek's often-cited examination (1987) of teacher perceptions regarding successful teaching, Graham's explanation (1986) of why students do not acquire motor skills as a result of participation in physical education, and the work of Orlick (1978, 1982) and Kohn (1992) provide objective evidence that such questionable practices are rampant. Although recent and significant national attempts have been made to improve the quality of physical education (e.g., NASPE Outcomes Project and Developmentally Appropriate Physical Education Practices for Children), the question remains whether these efforts will stimulate change at the gymnasium level. Another factor adding to the dilemma of achieving quality physical education programming is that many physical education programs are personality-driven, not program-driven: Dedicated teachers work hard at developing quality programs, but some teachers do not.

A Time to Reflect—Questions About Tomorrow and Quality Physical Education

1. Should instructional decisions reflect the major professional responsibility of developing quality programs?

2. Will large group competitive activities that neither challenge skilled students nor accommodate for those less skilled cease to be the standard curriculum?

3. How long can large class size be used as an excuse not to plan, teach, and evaluate lessons?

4. Can physical educators rally behind a finite set of goals so expectations can be clearly defined? Can we honor and reward those who meet or surpass expectations?

5. When will those responsible for the profession realize they are all part of the same profession and not separate entities competing for identity and status?

6. Can physical education teachers begin to understand that losing in competitive activities does not increase learning, motivation, and willingness to work harder?

7. When will the affective domain be truly infused into curriculums? Will teachers realize that learning by one's self or against others cannot promote caring, sharing, empathy, cooperation, and trust?

8. When will physical education teachers begin to realize the power of cooperative learning in working toward quality physical education— even though these ideas may not match with personal experiences in sport and physical education?

9. When will teachers replace large group activities with partner and small group work so more students, not just the motor elite, can have access to learning opportunities, instruction, and the enjoyment derived from successful participation in physical activity?

10. Will physical education continue to exist as is? Will physical education cease to exist because too many refuse to try to create a new and different kind of physical education? Or, will physical education be a rightful partner in education by providing quality learning experiences that "warm the heart" rather than leave long lasting negative memories?

The Fable of the Hundredth Monkey

This intriguing fable (Keys, 1982) tells a story about creating change. It encourages us to work together toward a new and better day. It suggests that, together, many can—and do—make a difference.

On a small island, monkeys ate sweet potatoes that people left for them on the beach. The monkeys liked the taste of the raw sweet potatoes, but they found the sand unpleasant. A young female found she could solve the problem by washing the potatoes in a nearby stream. She taught this trick to her mother, and then her playmates, who in turn taught their mothers.

This cultural innovation was gradually picked up by the remaining young monkeys who learned to wash sweet potatoes and make them more palatable. Only the adults who imitated their children learned this social improvement. Other adults kept eating the dirty sweet potatoes.

As the story is told, something startling occurred. When the sun rose one day, 99 monkeys had learned to wash their sweet potatoes; later that morning, the hundredth monkey learned to wash potatoes, too. Then it happened! By that evening almost all of the monkeys were washing sweet potatoes before eating them. The added energy generated by this hundredth monkey washing sweet potatoes somehow created an ideological breakthrough.

Thus, when a certain critical number of individuals achieves and subsequently acts on a new awareness, this awareness and action may be communicated from one to another. Although the exact number may vary, the *hundredth monkey phenomenon* means that when only a limited number of people know of a better way of doing something, it may remain the property of only these people. But there is a point at which, if one more person tunes into and acts on the awareness, wider change occurs.

Students need your awareness and action to change and improve physical education through cooperative learning. You may be the "Hundredth Person." Will you furnish the added energy and action to create quality physical education for more students?

References

Graham, G. 1986. Motor skill acquisition—An essential goal of physical education. *Journal of Physical Education, Recreation and Dance* 58(7): 44-48.

Keys, K. 1982. *The hundredth monkey.* Coos Bay, OR: Vision Books.

Kohn, A. 1992. *No contest.* Boston: Houghton Mifflin.

Orlick, T. 1978. *The cooperative sports and games book.* New York: Pantheon.

———. 1982. *The second cooperative sports and games book.* New York: Pantheon.

Placek, J. 1987. Conceptions of success in teaching: Busy, happy, and good? In *Teaching in physical education,* edited by T. Templin and J. Olson, 46-55. Champaign, IL: Human Kinetics.

Ross, J., C. Dotson, G. Gilbert, and S. Katz. 1985. The national children and youth fitness study I: What are kids doing in school physical education? *Journal of Physical Education, Recreation and Dance* 56(1): 73-76.

Ross, J., R. Pate, C. Corbin, L. Delpy, and R. Gold. 1987. The national children and youth fitness study II: What is going on in the physical education program? *Journal of Physical Education, Recreation and Dance* 58(9): 78-84.

Index

About the Author

Steve Grineski, EdD, is a professor and program coordinator for elementary and developmental/adapted physical education at Moorhead State University, Moorhead, Minnesota.

Steve has more than 22 years of teaching experience—10 years in public school physical education and 12 years of teacher education in elementary and developmental/adapted physical education. He received the National Association for Sport and Physical Education Inspiration Award in 1994 and the MSU Academic Affairs Award for Excellence in Teaching in 1995.

Author of over 60 publications and articles about cooperative learning and physical education, Steve also has made more than 50 conference presentations, including sessions at the 1990 and the 1992 International Conference for the Study of Cooperation in Education.

Steve is a member of the International Association for the Study of Cooperation in Education, and the American Association of Health, Physical Education, Recreation and Dance. He also served on the editorial board for *Teaching Elementary Physical Education*.